The Plymouth Cookbook

RECIPES FROM AMERICA'S HOMETOWN

Restaurant Biographies by Louisa Clerici

Published by Moore Media, Inc., Plymouth, MA

ISBN-13: 978-0-692-16348-1

moore media, inc.

FOODIE
FEDERATION

List of Restaurants

The Plymouth Cookbook

❧ BREAKFAST ❧

Two slices of fluffy golden Texas-style French toast, layered with creamy lemony ricotta cheese, and topped with blueberry syrup.
Courtesy of The Bluebird Café.

The inside of this fluffy three-egg omelet is filled with portobello mushrooms, spinach, and creamy Monterey cheese. It's all topped off with homemade pico de gallo, sour cream, and sliced avocados.
Courtesy of Carmen's Café Nicole.

This perfectly poached and creamy egg sits atop slices of fresh avocado and homemade hummus, all piled onto airy, toasted chiabatta bread.
Courtesy of The Farmers Table.

Not sure if you want breakfast or lunch? Try this wonderful warm spinach salad with sautéed mushrooms and onions, crumbled feta, and fried eggs to top it off. Served with a light Asian dressing.
Courtesy of The Jolly Bean Cafe.

Two crispy coated, soft-boiled eggs served with roasted root veggie home fries and an arugula balsamic salad.
Courtesy of Local Yolk Company.

Two perfectly poached eggs topped with creamy hollandaise sauce, served over a bed of sautéed spinach, onions, mushrooms, and cheddar cheese.
Courtesy of Will & Co. Café.

❧ APPETIZERS ❧

Welcome to the Caribbean! Zesty marinated chicken wings cooked to a golden brown, are tossed in a sweet and tangy banana garlic sauce, along with fried plantains. Served with a tropical crème dipping sauce.
Courtesy of The Blue-Eyed Crab.

Tender chicken breast tossed with spicy Buffalo sauce, shredded carrots and celery, gorgonzola and Monterey Jack cheeses, all rolled in a wonton wrapper and fried to golden perfection.
Courtesy of The Speedwell Tavern.

Nuggets of smokey kielbasa and caramelized pineapple simmered in a sweet and spicy reduction sauce. The perfect snackin' or party food.
Courtesy of Surfside Smokehouse.

EST.D 1620

Cranberry Hummus .... page 63

Hummus done Plymouth style! Cranberry sauce in the hummus gives it tang, and a topping of dried cranberries and goat cheese make it decadent. Served with pita chips and fresh veggie sticks.
Courtesy of TAR BAR.

Stuffed Quahogs .... page 73

Chocked full of tender, fresh clam, with a subtle smokiness from the linguica, and the wonderful flavor of golden brown bread crumbs.
Courtesy of Waterfront Bar and Grill.

❧ LUNCH ❧

East Indian Dahl .... page 7

Creamy yellow split peas and aromatic curry, cumin, and ginger give this classic East Indian dish its appeal.
Courtesy of The Blue Blinds Bakery.

KKatie's Peppercorn Steak Burger .... page 29

Fresh, never frozen, Angus beef makes this one juicy burger, topped with bacon, caramelized onions, and bleu cheese, served on a fluffy onion brioche bun.
Courtesy of KKaties Burger Bar.

Autumn Scallop Salad .... page 39

Arugula topped with roasted pumpkin seeds, granola, goat cheese, plump cranberries, and fluffy seared sea scallops, with a cranberry vinaigrette.
Courtesy of Martini's Bar & Grill.

Peasecods (Savory Meat Pies) .... page 49

The savory ground meat filling in these little pies has hints of orange, cinnamon, ginger, and cloves. All surrounded by a flaky pastry crust. Enjoy comfort food done the Pilgrim way with this adapted 17th century recipe.
Courtesy of Plimoth Plantation.

Howland at the Spoon .... page 55

Bratwurst, aged Vermont cheddar cheese, and locally brewed beer. Need we say more? All your favorite comfort foods go into making this creamy, delicious soup.
Courtesy of Second Wind Brewing Co.

Wharf Clam Chowder .... page 65

Traditional New England clam chowder, thick and creamy, with subtle hints of thyme and parsley.
Courtesy of Tavern on the Wharf.

Road House Chili. .... page 67

The perfect blend of seasonings creates this flavorful and spicy, slow-cooked chili.
Courtesy of T-Bones Road House.

Homemade Fishcakes .... page 77

These melt-in-your-mouth, fried fishcakes have been a New England tradition for centuries. Now you'll know why. Served with your choice of cocktail or tartar sauce.
Courtesy of Wood's Seafood.

❧ DINNER ❧

ESTD 1620

New York–Style Garden Pesto Pizza . . . page 69

Tender yet crispy, thin-crust pizza topped with a delectable garlic-basil pesto sauce, and fresh tomatoes, artichoke hearts, mozzarella, and asiago cheeses.
Courtesy of Top Crust Pizza.

Colonial Meatloaf . . . . page 80

This classic favorite is packed with extra zippy flavor with the addition of BBQ sauce.
Courtesy of Cape Auto (surprise!).

❧ Sweets ❧

Guilty's Fruit & Oat Bar . . . . page 21

Tender crust made with oats and coconut flakes, topped with velvety raspberry jam, fresh berries, and crumbly streusel.
Courtesy of Guilty Bakery.

Bread Pudding . . . . page 33

This traditional bread pudding, made with brioche, gets a modern twist with the addition of fruit. Served warm with vanilla ice cream.
Courtesy of Leena's Kitchen.

Chocolate Chip Cookies . . . . page 45

Warm out of the oven, crispy on the outside, yet melty on the inside—the all-American cookie.
Courtesy of Piece of Cake.

Chocolate Espresso Cheesecake . . . . . . page 53

Luscious chocolate and espresso, with hints of orange and vanilla make this a cheesecake you won't forget.
Courtesy of Rye Tavern.

Orange-Cranberry Scones . . . . page 71

Crispy on the outside, tender and flakey inside, made with orange zest and Craisins for the perfect marriage of sweet and tart.
Courtesy of Water Street Café.

Deep-Fried Ice Cream . . . . page 79

Just the way it should be—crispy crunchy on the outside and cold and creamy on the inside.
Courtesy of Ziggy's Ice Cream & Food.

❧ Sides ❧

Cardamom & Golden Raisin Loaf . . . . page 23

This luscious airy bread with aromatic hints of cardamom and sweet golden raisins is just as good toasted with butter as it for making French toast.
Courtesy of Hearth Artisan Bread.

Ranch Dressing & Dry Rub . . . . page 37

A creamy dressing perfect for dipping. The versatile dry rub version is perfect for enhancing everything from veggies to wings!
Courtesy of Main Street Sports Bar & Grill.

Foreword

Chef Martha Timke

With a degree in culinary arts from Newbury College in Brookline, MA, Martha Timke has been a professional chef for more than 20 years, and has been teaching culinary arts for more than 10. While making a career as a pastry chef and specializing in wedding cakes, complex desserts, chocolate work, breakfast pastries, and yeast breads, Chef Timke also finds great satisfaction preparing all manners of savory foods. She worked her way to becoming the executive pastry chef at The Catered Affair in Norwell, MA, and has been a pastry and culinary chef at a variety of establishments throughout the Boston area. A highlight of her career was enjoying a position as an instructor and academic supervisor for the Pastry Program at The Cambridge School of Culinary Arts in Cambridge, MA. She's also had the pleasure of teaching culinary and pastry classes at Bristol Community College, Blue Hills Regional, Newbury College, Good Life Kitchen, and Crittenton Hastings House. Examples of her work can be seen at cedarcrestkitchen.com. Chef Timke is now living in Sarasota, FL, with her husband, Paul Justice, and their dog, Lexie. She currently holds the position of director of baking and pastry at The Center for Culinary Arts at Keiser University, Sarasota, FL.

In 1985 I was 25 and made a huge leap of faith. I left my home, New York City, its cultural richness and diversity, food, art, music, as well as my childhood, to move to Arlington, Massachusetts to get married.

My first dining experience there was a place called The Polynesian. Everything had pineapple in it! And chopsticks? What chopsticks! I was used to getting my favorite cold sesame noodles delivered from Empire Szechuan or running down to Cubanos y Chinos Coffee Shop (yes, Cuban *and* Chinese) for café con leche and rice and beans. As a teenager, the last of five at home, I often joined my parents out for a meal at the many and varied restaurants around the city, and at all hours of the day and night. Dim sum at midnight, anyone?

But back to Massachusetts. Let's just say, that in 1985, in my humble opinion, suburban Boston's food scene was a waste land. I was not a chef then. That came later, after children, divorce, and regular trips to New York to get my sesame noodle fix.

I moved to Randolph and I cooked, and learned, and eventually got my degree in culinary arts and became a working chef, and then an instructor. A good part of my career was spent at the prestigious The Catered Affair where I was the pastry chef. Eventually I took a position as academic supervisor of the Pastry Program at the Cambridge School of Culinary Arts and moved further south to Marshfield. Food was all around me, and as I moved farther south and my career grew, so did the food scene in Massachusetts.

(left to right) From the country cottage feel of Bramhall's Country Store, to the elegance of Mirbeau's Bistro & Wine Bar, to the spectacular views at the Surfside Smokehouse, Plymouth's restaurant scene has something to fit every taste.

"... THE PLYMOUTH FOOD SCENE HAS EXPLODED, AND ALTHOUGH THE CHOWDER IS STILL GOOD, THERE IS SO MUCH MORE!"

Now, living in Florida, people often ask me where I'm from. I say I'm from the South Shore. That's just what happens when you've lived somewhere, seen it change and grow for 30 years. It's been so gratifying for me to see my fellow chefs, students, protégés, and friends do so well and come so far. And I love being a local! Warming up at the bar with some chowder and a beer at a pub in Plymouth while the Pats are on—does it get any better than that?

Recently, though, the Plymouth food scene has exploded, and although the chowder is still good, there is so much more! The people coming to and living in Plymouth know food and expect a worldly experience, and the chefs of Plymouth are ready to deliver. Experienced chefs, shop owners, and restaurateurs are looking at food from different points of view and using their skills to present new and wonderful creations. Young chefs and bakers are coming in and making bold statements; coming to live and learn just like I did all those years ago.

This wonderful collection of recipes in *The Plymouth Cookbook* brings us just a sampling of how these chefs, bakers, and restaurateurs are making Plymouth into a true foodie destination. I can't wait to get my own copy so that, no matter where I am, I can have the South Shore with me in the kitchen always.

— *Chef Martha Timke, Director Baking and Pastry Program at Keiser University, Sarasota, FL*

Preface

The idea for *The Plymouth Cookbook* first came to me when I was on a foodie destination vacation in New Orleans. It seemed that every restaurant we went into had tables of local cookbooks for sale. Some were books of specific restaurants, and some were compilations of recipes from many restaurants in New Orleans. I thought, "Why hasn't anyone done this yet in Plymouth? Visitors to our special town would love to bring a cookbook home as a memento, and it would give the local restaurant community pride and appreciation."

So, having been in the textbook publishing industry for the past 25+ years, I know well what's involved with book production, especially the difficulties faced with a book that needs content gathered from many sources, rather than just one author. I knew this would be a big undertaking, so I shelved the idea, with intentions of coming back to it when I had more time. But when would that be? We all know what usually happens when you do this—nothing.

Flash forward a year or so later, and I'm having breakfast with my friend Louisa Clerici, and I happen to mention the cookbook idea. Well, being a foodie herself, she absolutely loved it, and said, "Well, you know I'm a writer, and I'd love to partner with you and make this happen."

Thus, the Foodie Federation was born! We spent months traveling from restaurant to restaurant in Plymouth, introducing the project and wrangling in the chefs to pull recipes out of their heads and commit them to paper— not an easy task! I learned a lot about the restaurant industry during the process, and saw firsthand the amount of time the owners and staff dedicate to their love of food. It truly is their lives 24/7 for many of them.

To the Plymouth restaurants: Thank you for letting us become part of your family, and sharing something personal with us in this book. And we certainly appreciated all the delicious meals we tasted along the way—a few extra pounds later, Louisa and I joke that, "It was a hard job, but someone had to do it!"

Also thank you to my friend, Louisa. This book probably would not have happened without you. Long live the Foodie Federation!

— *Vanessa Moore, Publisher, Moore Media, Inc., Plymouth, MA*

The Foodie Federation, Vanessa and Louisa, hard at work and always on the job.

As a child, I learned that cooking is a labor of love. My mom was a wonderful cook and she made everything from scratch. Sunday afternoons were filled with the delicious scents of chicken roasting, potatoes being whipped on the stovetop, and always a special dessert. I learned early how to bake and I was happy measuring, mixing, and taking batches of cookies out from the oven. I treasure my mother's cookbooks and memories of watching Julia Child with her. Julia brought humor and elegance to cooking.

Now as a therapist, I help people relax, sleep better, and make peace with food. Food nourishes our bodies, minds, and spirits. I feel honored to help clients learn to enjoy the benefits of joyful eating, and inspire them toward radiant health.

In a busy world, restaurants have attained a new prominence. Increasingly, restaurants are the places where people meet and fall in love, where families celebrate, where we enjoy the feasts of life. My personal history is woven together by wonderful restaurants. Tuesday nights at Ernie's in Plymouth, sharing pizza with my friends Steve and Debbie. I'll always remember Indian pudding at Durgin Park with my parents. My brother Larry and I had our first Fenway Franks at Fenway Park. I met my husband Rick in a South Shore restaurant. I fell in love with delis at Wolfie's in Miami with my in-laws. On a trip to New York City with my girlfriend Lynn, we splurged on one special meal at Windows on the World. From the top floor of the North Tower Building One of the original World Trade Center, we looked out onto the skyline of Manhattan. I recall the joy of sitting at that table with a magical view of the whole world.

When my very creative friend Vanessa Moore first told me her idea for this book, I felt instantly excited. I could not have found a more fun foodie than Vanessa to share this journey and celebrate Plymouth as a foodie destination. This jazzed me as a writer and a foodie. Food is story. I feel privileged to have had the opportunity to hear the stories of Plymouth's finest restaurants, and am thrilled to share them in this book.

— *Louisa Clerici, Therapist, Clear Mind Systems, Plymouth, MA, www.clearmindsystems.net*
  and Writer of Fiction, Articles, Freelance

Dedicated to Anthony Bourdain.

A portion of the sale proceeds from this book will be donated
to fighting addiction and depression through local charities and causes.

The Plymouth Cookbook

RECIPES FROM AMERICA'S HOMETOWN

Alden Park

Alden Park Bar and Grill is a festival of variety. The menu here is so versatile and enticing; you won't have any problem finding exactly what you want. If you're in a seafood mood, the maple salmon served with jasmine rice and asparagus has a delicious maple sauce and balsamic glaze. Or if you're craving meat, try the slow-roasted braised short ribs, which are melt-in-your-mouth heaven, and perfectly paired with garlic mashed potatoes and baby carrots. One look at this menu and you'll start planning a return visit. Executive Chef Adnilson Oliveira excels at creative comfort food. The menu changes several times a year and weekly specials are a nice surprise and exactly what you're craving. This is contemporary American cuisine taken to the next level.

Appetizers and salads are elevated here. Try the chickpea fries with roasted tomato aioli, asiago, and truffle oil. The roasted red and yellow stacked beets are amazing. Lunch ranges from a mouth-watering eggplant Parmesan to a tuna melt stuffed with roasted red peppers, fontina cheese, arugula, and tomato. There are vegetarian options and 70 percent of the menu can be made gluten-free. Dinner entrees include Mediterranean panko cod, an amazing stuffed meatloaf, and the spectacular Seafood Lover with shrimp, scallops, and lobster tail.

Alden Park is located in the Colony Place shopping mall. Though once you enter this sophisticated restaurant, you forget about the stores and shopping. You've entered an elegant dining room rivaling anything Boston has to offer. Walt Wunder and his staff have created a culinary sanctuary. Comfy booths, a happening bar, and a stylish outdoor patio with true ambiance, including a unique water-fire fountain, add to the relaxing vibe. Alden Park is a perfect place for craft cocktails, a romantic dinner, or a night out with friends. The large function room is a great place for parties, as well. And do not leave here without trying one of the divine desserts. The banana bread grilled cheese—house-made banana bread, creamy mascarpone, bananas Foster sauce, and vanilla ice cream—is scrumptious and just one of the reasons a visit to Alden Park Bar and Grill is unforgettable.

Alden Park

160 Colony Place, Plymouth, MA 02360

Hours: Sun–Tue, 11:30AM–9:00PM
Wed–Sat, 11:30AM–9:00PM

aldenparkrestaurant.com

508-830-6777

THE SEAFOOD LOVER

DIRECTIONS

1. Boil the lobster in a stock pot for approximately 8 minutes. Remove the lobster from the water, and when cool enough to handle, remove the meat from the claws, knuckles, and tail. You may split the tail lengthwise and place the meat back into the shell to create a dynamic presentation, as in the picture. Set aside.

2. Heat the oil in a sauté pan over medium heat. Add the remaining ingredients, except the pasta. Stir for just a few minutes until the shrimp and scallops are almost cooked through.

3. Add the lobster meat to the pan. Cover and allow the sauce to reduce a bit.

4. While sauce is reducing, cook your pasta.

5. Place the cooked pasta in a shallow bowl, and top with the seafood sauce. Finish with the split tail placed on top, and a fresh orchid for a lovely presentation.

Serves 1.

INGREDIENTS

1 live lobster

¼ C olive oil

1 tsp garlic, minced

3 shrimp, shelled and cleaned

3 jumbo-sized scallops, cleaned

10 snow peas

8 medley tomatoes

¼ C sliced button mushrooms

pinch salt and pepper, to taste

¼ C white wine

1 T butter

4 oz fettuccine pasta

The Bluebird Café

The Bluebird Café has a great down-home feeling that hungry customers always crave. Cozy and comfortable, you'll feel happy here dining at a comfy table, or at the counter, swiveling on a chrome stool. There's a diner-like mood from the moment you're greeted as you come in the door. This is down-home cooking here, but elevated. Simple, yet creative.

Owners Annette and Tim White use locally sourced food when available. They buy from farmers' markets, ingredients with no additives. You'll find eggs from the farm, homemade bread, and they cook with real butter on the grill top. You'll want to try the straightforward homemade hash and eggs, a good-for-you veggie omelette, or maybe a traditional Belgian waffle with fresh strawberries and caramelized bananas. Lemon ricotta pancakes are lovely and delectable. Or maybe spice it up a bit with a Bluebird Benny—grilled cornbread topped with their smokin' pulled pork, poached eggs, hollandaise, and sriracha sauce. Their own smoked meats are a specialty on many dishes. Chase it down with a wonderful cup of coffee from hometown Plymouth roaster, Speedwell Coffee.

Kids and adults both love the bird in a nest—two eggs dropped inside grilled bread with bacon. The café is located on Big Saby's Pond, next to the Ellis Haven Campground and kids delight in watching the ducks, bunnies, and even an occasional peacock stroll by the pond and campground. The whole family will enjoy the Elvis cakes—two large pancakes filled with peanut butter, topped with bananas Foster sauce and chocolate chips—pure happiness in a breakfast dish!

Lunch here is comforting and excellent. There are specials here on the board every day, Tim's recipes. But Tim and Annette are always on the lookout for what's trending in the restaurant world, what customers are enjoying, and then putting their own individual spin on the dish. Recent specials include oatmeal-almond pancakes, BBQ ribs and eggs, and Lemon-Ricotta Stuffed French Toast. Don't miss the blueberry muffins and daily desserts made from scratch. Stop by the cheerful Bluebird Café, you'll be happy you did.

The Bluebird Café

531 Federal Furnace Road,
Plymouth, MA 02360

Hours: Daily, 6:30AM–2:00PM
Closed Tuesdays

gotothebluebirdcaf.wixsite.com/mysite

508-927-2653

LEMON-RICOTTA
STUFFED FRENCH TOAST

DIRECTIONS

1. Whisk together ricotta, lemon zest, lemon extract, and agave. Set aside.

2. In a mixing bowl, combine the buttermilk, eggs, vanilla, cinnamon, and salt.

3. In a skillet, over medium heat, melt the butter. Add sugar and cook about 3 minutes.

4. Dip the Texas toast in the egg mixture to coat well. Add toast slices to the hot skillet and cook 3 minutes on each side, or until golden brown.

5. While toast is frying, in another saucepan, melt the butter for the blueberry sauce. Add the sugar and blueberries. Heat until the sugar is melted, about 3 minutes, then take off heat.

6. Lay toast on a plate and spread ricotta mixture over each piece. Stack toasts, two per person (or more if you like!), and top with blueberry sauce. Sprinkle with confectioners' sugar and a few more fresh blueberries.

Serves 4.

TIP: The Bluebird Café uses duck eggs in the egg mixture, which produces a fluffier toast outcome. Give it a try!

INGREDIENTS

½ C ricotta cheese

zest of one lemon

½ tsp lemon extract

1 T agave

¾ C buttermilk

2 eggs

½ tsp vanilla extract

¼ tsp cinnamon

¼ tsp salt

2 T butter

¼ C sugar

8 slices Texas toast

confectioners' sugar for garnish

BLUEBERRY SAUCE:

2 T butter

1 T sugar

1 C fresh blueberries

The Blue Blinds Bakery

The beautifully restored building on North Street in downtown Plymouth is a culinary jewel that harkens back to Plymouth past. Originally owned by Mayflower voyager John Cook, the building became a restaurant in 1940, and then was meticulously restored many years later, re-opening under the original name in the midst of the historic district. The scent of organic bread baking, pies and muffins cooling, and rich coffee brewing welcomes you as you climb the porch stairs and enter this lovely piece of history. In the summer, the porch is filled with diners deep in conversation. In the cold weather, the fire greets you as you enter, and the delicate sounds of instrumental folk music seem like a soundtrack to the colorful murals of the original settlers and their harrowing journey. Soon, the Blue Blinds Bakery will open another restaurant, The Yellow Deli, on Main Street.

There are shelves of fresh artisan breads, and dishes of scones and sweet rolls. In glass cases, cakes and pies call out to you. The peach crumb pie is not to be missed. There's locally roasted coffee and espresso along with organic teas and chai. A refreshing hibiscus fruit cooler will turn a hot summer morning cool and spicy. There are wonderful breakfast plates of pancakes, golden waffles, and French toast with fresh fruit and real maple syrup. Customers swoon over the eggs and cheddar on specialty bread, or go lighter with organic granola and yogurt. Lunch is all about hearty soups, available in a sourdough bread bowl. Blue Blinds has provided us with the recipe for their delicious East Indian Dahl, available in the winter, wonderful with one of their sandwiches. Even the simple grilled cheese is everything a grilled cheese should be, and then some.

The Boston Globe called Blue Blinds, "probably the prettiest, all-around most pleasing café south of Boston." There is a simplicity and reverence that reflects the welcoming ways of the owners and staff and their spiritual community. From their respect for good, quality foods and organic baked goods, to the relaxing atmosphere of the cozy dining room, Blue Blinds Bakery is an outstanding experience in quality, delicious dining, and superb service.

The Blue Blinds Bakery

7 North Street, Plymouth, MA 02360
Hours: Mon–Thur, 6:00AM–9:00PM
Fri, 6:00AM–3:00PM; Sun, 7:00AM–9:00PM
Closed Saturdays
blueblindsbakery.com
508-747-0462

EAST INDIAN DAHL

DIRECTIONS

1. Rinse split peas well. Simmer the peas in the water in a thick-bottom pot, until soft and pasty, stirring often, about 30–40 minutes (time will vary depending on the peas and water temperature).

2. Blend garlic and ginger together with a little water, then sauté, along with all other ingredients, except spinach, in a frying pan, until onions are tender.

3. Add this mixture to the cooked split peas and stir together.

4. Chop spinach and add to soup. Mix well.

Serve topped with some chopped cilantro or parsley. Serves 10–12.

FOODIE FACT

Curry powder, which originated on the Indian subcontinent, is actually a blend of spices including coriander, turmeric, cumin, fenugreek, and chili peppers. Curry dishes are now found worldwide. Depending on the country where it is used, additional ingredients such as ginger, garlic, fennel seed, caraway, cinnamon, clove, mustard seed, cardamom, nutmeg, white turmeric, curry leaf, long pepper, and black pepper may also be included. This is why a curry dish from Jamaica, for example, will be very different from a curry dish from China.

INGREDIENTS

4½ C yellow split peas, dry

14 C water

2–3 cloves fresh garlic, to taste

2 T fresh ginger

¼ C sunflower oil

2 C onions, diced

½ T ground cumin

½ T ground coriander

1 tsp ground turmeric

pinch of cayenne, to taste

1 tsp curry powder

1 T salt

4 C fresh spinach, chopped

fresh cilantro or parsley for garnish

The Blue-Eyed Crab

Locals and visitors to Plymouth no longer need to take a trip to the islands for some great Caribbean food. The innovative menu at The Blue-Eyed Crab will immediately put you in a tropical mood. The colorful dining room and casual bar shine with an island ambiance. Eating on the outdoor patio overlooking the harbor in the sparkling sunlight invites you to kick back and enjoy some of the best food Plymouth has to offer.

Chef Jim Casey has created a dynamic menu filled with fresh seafood and island treats you'll find nowhere else. Order a variety of small plates so you can try everything. From the coconut bay scallops with orange chile marmalade to the lobster and lump crab creole over toasted bread, each creation is a feast of flavor. The jerk chicken buns with melted Gouda cheese, key lime aioli, and mango salsa are unforgettable. Chef Casey was generous to give us his recipe for Banana Garlic Chicken Wings with tropical Crème Dip and Sweet Plantains, a signature dish. Whether you're here for lunch or a night out, it's all about color here, yellow walls, red dishes, and vibrant, delicious food you'll rave about.

Big plates, available after 5:00PM, include the delicate baked corn crumb and crab crusted cod with tropical rice, seasonal vegetables, and sherry ginger butter; and grilled Jamaican pepper steak tips with sautéed onions and peppers, grilled avocado, whipped potatoes, and seasonal vegetables. The Blue-Eyed Crab's fish-of-the-day is served with your choice of a topper and you'll want to try them all—black bean cucumber salsa, pickled onion slaw, or pineapple-lime jelly taste incredible on seafood fresh from the ocean. All served with their special homemade cornbread.

Cocktails here are innovative and beautiful. Try a breezy, lime in the coconut—Cruzan coconut rum, coconut, and lime with a spiced rum float—"Don't Worry, Be Happy," in a glass!

Jim and Heather Casey have created a unique and exciting restaurant, inspired by an island cafe, but taken to the next level, one of the Food Network's Top Places to Eat.

The Blue-Eyed Crab
Caribbean Grill & Rum Bar

170 Water Street (at Village Landing),
Plymouth, MA 02360

Hours: Sun–Thur, 11:30AM–9:00PM
Fri & Sat, 11:30AM–10:00PM

blue-eyedcrab.com

508-747-6776

BANANA GARLIC CHICKEN WINGS
WITH TROPICAL CRÈME DIP & SWEET PLANTAINS

INGREDIENTS

10 lb chicken wings

4 ripe, yellow plantains

2 qt canola oil

MARINADE:

4 T grated ginger

2 tsp jalapeño, chopped

3 pieces star anise

3 cinnamon sticks

$2/3$ C soy sauce

$2/3$ C orange juice

1½ tsp garlic, chopped

6 tsp granulated sugar

BANANA GARLIC SAUCE:

8 tsp garlic, minced   zest of ½ an orange

3 T butter   juice of 1 orange

1 C Asian fish sauce   ½ C sweet chili sauce

1 C real maple syrup   2 bananas, sliced

1 C orange juice   1½ oz banana liquor

TROPICAL CRÈME DIP:

18 oz pineapple juice

¼ C granulated sugar

1 qt sour cream

NOTE: Serves a party of about 20.

DIRECTIONS

1. Combine all marinade ingredients and pour over the 10 lb of raw chicken wings. Marinate in refrigerator overnight.

2. The next day, remove wings from marinade and place on a baking sheet. Roast in a 350° oven for 30 minutes. Let cool, then set aside in refrigerator.

3. Next, make the Banana Garlic Sauce. Toast the garlic in butter in a large sauce pot for 15 minutes on low heat, until it is a dark golden brown.

4. Add the rest of the sauce ingredients. Bring to a boil and then simmer for 20 minutes. Puree everything in a blender. Set aside.

5. Next, make the Tropical Crème Dipping Sauce. In a small sauce pot, reduce the pineapple juice and sugar down to about one-third, or 6 ounces. This will take

about 30 minutes. It should be slightly caramelized. Then set aside to chill in refrigerator for 1 hour.

6. Add reduced juice mixture to the sour cream and mix. Set aside in refrigerator.

7. Now it's time to fry the plantains. Cut the two ends off the plaintains, then carefully peel them. Cut into ½-inch slices. Deep fry in 350° oil for 3 minutes. Set aside.

8. Finally, assemble the dish. Grill the pre-roasted wings until they are golden brown. Meanwhile, heat up the Banana Garlic Sauce in a stock pot. When the wings are done, add them and the fried plantains into the sauce and toss until everything is glazed and very hot.

9. Serve on a platter with the Tropical Crème Dip in a bowl on the side.

Bramhall's Country Store

Just five minutes from Plymouth Harbor and a short walk from Plimoth Plantation you turn a corner and feel as though you're in the middle of Vermont. Bramhall's Country Store, a 1750-era bright red saltbox is part of why we call Plymouth, "America's Hometown." George Bramhall bought the building from Nathaniel Carver in 1828 for just $25. Like the famous rock and the sparkling blue harbor, Bramhall's has endured, run by the same family since 1828.

This country store is a foodie destination for folks from miles around. The summer opens to lines of customers hungry for the first Bramhall's lobster roll of the season. On any beautiful summer day you can see families sitting around picnic tables, under the shade of graceful linden trees. Veggie wraps, lobster grilled cheese, and their special lobster tacos with amazing homemade tortillas are popular. For their tortillas, Bramhall's uses local corn that has been nixtamalized, milled, pressed, and cooked in-house by one of the Plimoth Grist Mill millers. Save room for a waffle cone filled with Ben & Jerry's® ice cream. Bramhall's is one of the only unfranchised Ben & Jerry's® scoop shops left in the world.

The air is filled with the laughter of children, and the satisfied oohs and aahs of hungry diners. Everyone seems to know each other. And in five minutes, you'll know the whole family even if it's your first visit. Brother and sister Ben Bramhall and Sally Bramhall run this landmark, along with help from siblings Sam and Liz and mom Jami. This is a family business run by people who obviously love to take care of their customers and friends.

Bramhall's has continued their tradition of supporting local farms. In back, there is a farm stand with fresh produce—baskets of strawberries and bushels of corn along with cold cases filled with artisan cheese and other specialties. On a hot day, the cold smoothies and organic iced teas soothe and cool the soul. On many Tuesdays, the old red house rings with the songs of the open mic with music played by local musicians. Bramhall's is simply a delicious destination where a community celebrates fine food and company, makes friends of visitors, and fills the summer and fall to the brim with goodness.

Bramhall's Country Store
2 Sandwich Road, Plymouth, MA 02360
Hours: Daily, 11:00AM–8:00PM, seasonally
bramhallscountrystore.com
508-746-1844

Lobster Tacos

DIRECTIONS

1. Thinly slice a scallion, and set aside. (Feel free to substitute spring onion, fresh onion, or cured onion as the season progresses.)

2. In a bowl, add water to the masa and salt (optional), just enough so that the dough should cohere without sticking to your fingers. Roll into golf-ball-sized chunks.

3. Press the masa balls with a tortilla press, or flatten with a rolling pin to $1/8$-inch. Cook in cast iron pan over medium-high heat. Flip after 10 seconds and then cook each side for 1–2 minutes more. Wrap finished tortillas in a clean towel and set aside in a warm oven at the lowest temp, or in an oven warming drawer.

4. Steam or boil the lobster. When cool enough to handle, shuck the lobster and remove all the meat. Coarsley chop.

5. Remove the tortillas from their warming place, and put on your serving plates.

6. Smear jalapeño cream cheese, or other spreadable soft cheese of choice, over the warm tortillas. Add the lobster meat. Sprinkle the scallion over the lobster, and drizzle with melted butter.

Garnish with fresh cilantro and lime wedges, and enjoy! Serves 2.

INGREDIENTS

1 scallion

1½ C masa harina (corn flour)

dash salt (optional)

water

1 lobster

jalapeño cream cheese, or other spreadable soft cheese of choice

1 T melted butter

chopped cilantro, for garnish

quartered lime wedges, for garnish

Carmen's Café Nicole

Walking north on Water Street toward Café Nicole as you pass their free parking lot, you see the Café's outdoor terrace and immediately want to eat in this delightfully private outdoor haven. Though walking south on Water Street, you first see the Café's huge front windows and long to eat inside looking out on Plymouth Bay. Inside or outside, Carmen's Café Nicole is a perfect spot to dine in and muse on the beauty of the ocean.

Café Nicole has something of a dual flavor. The menu reflects on their love for both delicious American traditional café food and a wonderful and beautifully prepared selection of Mexican favorites. There aren't many restaurants where one diner can select authentic Mexican dishes like enchiladas de carne or chimichangas, while another can have an all-American burger or a Pilgrim turkey wrap. This restaurant reflects the diversity of our palates and the quality and authenticity of both American and Mexican foods—the best of both worlds.

Of course, American food at the seashore should always include well-prepared and fresh seafood. Café Nicole has a great variety including a shrimp and scallop combo and whole clams. The fish is fresh and comes from the ocean right across the road. The lunch menu also has a whole section of wraps like the Tuscan chicken, po-boy, green goddess, and the now-famous Carmenuch wrap (with grilled Italian sausage, provolone, onions, peppers, and ricotta).

And Café Nicole is a great place for breakfast. Many locals end their morning walks here and spend a while with the festive breakfast menu. You might enjoy your seaside Plymouth breakfast or fantasize that you're in Acapulco. Café Nicole has all the wonderful American dishes of hash and eggs, biscuits and gravy, and a selection of specialty omelets, including the wonderful Savory California Omelet. The recipe shared here is a delightful combination of baby spinach, portabella mushrooms, and fresh sliced avocado. On the other side of the border, there are huevos rancheros and Santa Maria tostada. The Café Nicole has a full bar with specialty drinks to top off this rich experience.

Carmen's Café Nicole

114 Water Street, Plymouth, MA 02360

Hours: Daily, 7:00AM–3:00PM

carmenscafenicole.com

508-747-4343

SAVORY CALIFORNIA OMELET

DIRECTIONS

1. Chop all the pico de gallo ingredients, and toss together in a bowl. Set aside.

2. In another bowl, whisk together the eggs and pinch of salt and pepper. Set aside.

3. Heat 1 tsp of the olive oil in a non-stick skillet, over medium heat. When hot, add the spinach and mushrooms, and a pinch of salt and pepper. Sauté for just a minute or two, then remove to a bowl and set aside.

4. Add the remaining 1 tsp oil to the skillet. When hot, add your beaten eggs. Stir briefly, then let sit untouched.

5. In a few minutes, the omelet will begin to solidify. (If there is too much liquid in the center, tilt the pan to distribute liquid to the sides.) With a rubber spatula, start lifting the edge of the omelet, moving around the edge of the entire pan. Gently keep prying and shaking the pan to completely loosen the omelet.

6. When loosened, add the cheese, then the mushrooms and spinach. Gently fold the omelet in half and let sit untouched for 30–60 seconds.

7. Slide the omelet onto your serving plate, top with the sliced avocado, and serve with the fresh pico de gallo and sour cream on the side.

Makes 1 large omelet. Serve with your favorite sides, such as hash browns, toast, black beans, or fruit.

INGREDIENTS

3 eggs

pinch salt and pepper

2 tsp olive oil

1 big handful of fresh baby spinach

1 C portobello mushrooms, sliced

1 C Monterey Jack cheese, shredded

half an avocado, sliced

sour cream

PICO DE GALLO:

1 medium red onion

1 medium tomato

half a fresh jalapeño, seeded

two sprigs of fresh cilantro

1 scallion

dash garlic powder

dash salt and pepper, to taste

Dillon's Local

At Dillon's Local they say you're only a stranger once, and they really mean it. After working in the restaurant industry for decades, Colin and Samantha Dillon decided to open the kind of pub where they would like to hang out. They've put their experience to work and created a casual, relaxing restaurant with delicious, creative food that continues to surprise and delight.

Whenever possible, ingredients are locally sourced, so wonderfully fresh food is served here. Littlenecks out of Buzzards Bay are just one of the ingredients that are making their seafood dishes special. The menu here changes seasonally and Chef Jeff Chevalier ("Chevy") has a special talent for innovative, mouth-watering fare. It's not surprising that this restaurant continues to win awards and was voted Best Lunch Spot 2017 by *South Shore Living Magazine*.

It's hard to choose just one appealing appetizer. Their crab cakes—two pan-seared lump crab cakes over a bed of arugula with a side of Cajun remoulade is simple and luscious. The baked ricotta dip—whipped ricotta cheese, Parmesan crust, white truffle oil, and crostini is a dish you'll crave again and again. Even a simple sandwich here is elevated. The Reubens here are perfect—cured brisket, braised red cabbage, Gruyère cheese, Russian dressing on grilled marble rye. Or how about a Cape Cod Reuben—flash-fried local cod, Gruyère cheese, house slaw, Russian dressing on grilled rye—a tempting twist on a traditional dish.

Their recipe for Portuguese Cod would even sparkle in Lisbon—oven-roasted cod, littlenecks, linguiça, corn, potatoes in a white wine clam broth. Don't miss trying the panko and herb-encrusted salmon with roasted beet coulis. Bourbon steak tips are amazing and swordfish is served with a limoncello butter that is just right. The comfort food vibe here continues with excellent pizzas and a yummy shepherd's pie. Just add a hand-crafted specialty cocktail and save room for dessert. Deana Leary bakes a wonderful key lime pie and Irish crème tiramisu. Sunday brunch on the outdoor deck or delicious food inside the cozy pub—you'll feel at home at Dillon's Local.

Dillon's Local

21 So. Park Avenue, Plymouth, MA 02360

Hours: Mon–Sat, 11:30AM–1:00AM
Sun, 10:00AM–1:00AM

dillonslocalplymouth.com

774-404-7913

DILLON'S LOCAL
— PLYMOUTH MA —

PORTUGUESE COD

DIRECTIONS

1. Preheat oven to 400°.
2. Add the oil to a sauté pan over medium heat. When hot, add the onion and celery and cook until translucent, about 4 minutes.
3. Add the littlenecks to the pan and sauté for 3–4 minutes more, stirring gently but constantly.
4. Add the linguiça and cook for 1 minute more, then deglaze with a bit of white wine.
5. Add the corn, cream, clam juice, and potatoes to the pan, cover loosely, and simmer on low for 10–12 minutes.
6. Place cod fillets in a baking pan, dot with pieces of the butter and pour remainder of the white wine into the pan. Bake for 10–12 minutes.
7. Take the cod out of the oven, and place each fillet in a shallow bowl. Place four littlenecks around each piece of cod, then spoon some chowder over it all.

Serves 2. Serve with a loaf of your favorite crusty bread to sop up the wonderful rustic chowder!

INGREDIENTS

2 tsp olive oil

$^1/_8$ C onion

$^1/_8$ C celery

8 littleneck clams

4 oz linguiça, sliced on bias

2 oz white wine, plus more for deglazing

1 ear of cooked corn kernels

½ C cream

6 oz clam juice

2 Yukon gold potatoes, cut into ¼-inch dice

2 (6-oz) cod fillets

2 T butter

1 loaf crusty bread

East Bay Grille

East Bay Grille is a fine restaurant that draws its loyal clientele from the entire South Shore. This wonderful establishment bridges the classic and contemporary, the classy and the casual. In summer, the sprawling outdoor patio and large covered bar bring the Grille's classy environment out to the water's edge, and can double the restaurant's capacity. Live entertainment and various events often make the patio and bar bristle with fun and energy. The outdoor bar is a favorite after-work meeting place and business destination.

From the white-shirted waitstaff and valet attendants to the culinary staff and bar crew, there is a feel of genuine professionalism. And from the greeting at the door to the impeccable service, you soon realize that this restaurant runs like a finely tuned machine.

Executive Chef Joel Mantel has created a menu that emphasizes classic recipes with tasteful hints of modern cuisine. Each dish is perfectly prepared, generously portioned, and pleases the palate without being pretentious. Chef Mantel gave us the recipe for East Bay Grille's popular Town Wharf Sirloin. This dish features a charbroiled center-cut sirloin with sweet caramelized onions and crumbled bleu cheese. This savory dish plays just the right flavor notes.

The menu has a seafood selection that stretches from fish and chips, baked scrod, and stuffed shrimp to seafood risotto, blackened salmon, and swordfish piccata. Diners drive for miles to have the perfect lobster roll, broiled scallops, and the Jamaican Arctic char. The traditional turkey dinner, or "Best of the Bird," is a dinner you've dreamed about if you're a turkey lover. The selection of steaks and chops is huge and top of the line. The chowder is amazing and the salads are impeccable. There is a substantial lunch menu with smaller versions of traditional plates, along with burgers, excellent sandwiches, and a long list of delicious appetizers.

East Bay Grille also specializes in functions, parties, and catering. The outdoor function area can handle up to 200 attendees. Dining at the East Bay Grille is a memorable experience, and a culinary delight.

East Bay Grille

173 Water Street, Plymouth, MA 02360

Hours: Daily, 11:00AM–1:00AM

eastbaygrille.com

508-746-9751

TOWN WHARF SIRLOIN

DIRECTIONS

1. Over low heat, saute the onions in the olive oil and butter, stirring every few minutes, until caramelized. As soon as the onions start sticking to the pan, let them stick a little to brown, but then stir them before they burn. Add a bit more oil, if you find the onions are on the verge of burning. This will take about 20–30 minutes. When done, set aside.

2. Heat your indoor gas range grill-top or outdoor grill up to grilling temperature.

3. Salt and pepper your steak. Brush with olive oil and charbroil for 4–5 minutes on each side.

4. Remove steak from grill and place on a cooking sheet. Top with the caramelized onions, then the crumbled bleu cheese. Place in a heated oven for 1–2 minutes, until cheese begins to melt.

5. Heat the demi-glace and spread in the center of your serving plate. Carefully place the steak atop the sauce, and serve.

Serves 1.

INGREDIENTS

¾ C Vidalia onions, sliced

1 tsp olive oil

1 tsp butter

14 oz center-cut sirloin steak

salt and pepper, to taste

2 oz bleu cheese
(Great Hill brand if possible)

2 oz Cabernet demi-glace

The Farmers Table

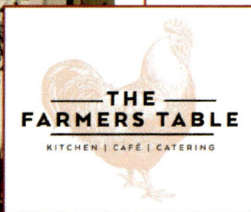

The Farmers Table captures the beauty of a quintessential New England farmhouse with antique furniture, high ceilings, and shiplap walls. Mother and daughter team, Lynn and Olivia Tripp, opened the café in 2016, locating it in Redbrook, the new community known as "the New England village reimagined." The Farmers Table is an integral part of Redbrook, where 1,200 new homes are tucked amid 1,400 acres of preserved forest, cranberry bogs, and ponds, and each home is within a short stroll of this cozy farm-to-table café.

Mother Lynn and daughter Olivia exude a joy that comes from a shared dream. Lynn is an associate professor at Johnson & Wales University, College of Culinary Arts in Providence, and Olivia is a graduate of the school with a degree in culinary nutrition. They are dedicated to farm-to-table cooking but also passionate about creating healthy food. It shows right away in the breakfast menu. Start with a delicious smoothie. The Immunity Booster is blended with spinach, orange, lemon, ginger, honey, flax, and chia. The breakfast sandwiches are hearty, but healthy. The Pilgrim—eggs, turkey bacon, cranberry mayo, American cheese, garden lettuce, and tomato—is served on sourdough bread baked by Hearth Artisan Bread in Plymouth. Their special Avocado Toast layers avocado, hummus, and a poached egg on ciabatta toast, so good you'll wish you could have it every morning.

A simple country lunch is elevated here. Start with the delightful grilled watermelon and fennel salad—grilled watermelon (lightly grilling brings out its natural juicy flavor) with fennel, feta, arugula, baby kale, sunflower seeds, and their house-made vinaigrette. The grilled chicken salad sandwich has that grilled caramelized sweetness with a little zip from red onion. It may be like no chicken salad you've ever had before! Desserts here are just like your grandmother made, if she was an incredible baker. Choose the special of the day—could be Boston cream pie, Key lime pie, or their unforgettable apple pie. Corn and fruit muffins, cookies, and scones are all a dessert-lover's dream. With a full-service bar and patio, dining at The Farmers Table is an exceptional experience.

The Farmers Table

1 Greenside Way N., Plymouth, MA 02360

Hours: Daily, 8:00AM–3:00PM
(except closed on Tuesdays);
Weekend Brunch, 9:00AM–1:00PM

farmerstableplymouth.com

508-224-2400

Poached Egg over Avocado Toast

DIRECTIONS

1. First, make the hummus. Soak the chickpeas overnight in water. (Or, you may use one 16-oz can of chickpeas, drained.)

2. Combine the chickpeas with the rest of the hummus ingredients, except the salt and pepper, in a food processor and blend until smooth. Taste, and adjust to your liking with salt and pepper. Set aside in refrigerator until ready to use.

3. Toast one slice of ciabatta bread.

4. Spread about 2 T of hummus onto the toasted bread.

5. Layer some arugula on top of the hummus.

6. Slice the avocado and layer it over the arugula.

7. Add the vinegar to a pot of water and bring to a simmer. Carefully crack the egg into the simmering water and poach for 3 minutes.

8. With a slotted spoon, carefully remove the poached egg from the water, letting any water drain off, and place on top of the avocado. Sprinkle with red pepper flakes, salt, and pepper to your liking.

Serves 1.

INGREDIENTS

ciabatta bread

arugula

1 egg

1 avocado

1 T white vinegar

red pepper flakes

salt and pepper, to taste

HUMMUS:

1½ C dried chickpeas

2 T tahini

1 C olive oil

¼ C lemon juice

1 T roasted garlic, chopped

salt and pepper, to taste

Guilty Bakery

One visit to this exceptional bakery and you'll find yourself "guilty" of looking for excuses to return. This jewel of a shop is a little slice of heaven in a bakery. It engages all the senses as you walk through the door. The sweet scent of butter cream icings and chocolate ganache, the pretty glass cases filled with a wonderland of delicate pastries—you can almost taste the goodness even before you reach for that first cupcake.

Pastry Chefs Amy and Krista put caring and quality into every detail of this shop and it's so much fun to watch them create and bake in the open kitchen. Everything is made from scratch and Amy believes that if you're going to allow yourself dessert in this calorie-conscious world, it should be something luxurious and ultra-delicious. Crave-worthy these pastries are, from whoopie pies and chocolate cream pie brownies to their famous Fruit & Oat Bars (a versatile dessert that can be made with different fruits). The creativity of Amy and Krista give us so many choices, you'll look forward to your next visit just to try one more…or maybe two…guilty!

The French macarons are spectacular and there are many special flavors of this light, almond meringue cookie—each bite, a little taste of pistachio or mint, or maybe hot chocolate or red velvet. Their classic macarons are well-known for their simplicity and burst of vanilla or coffee to savor. Guilty's signature cake—a white cake filled with white chocolate mousse and French macarons—is the stuff of legends.

A secret only the locals know: On Sunday mornings, they bake donuts. You'd better get there early, they sell out fast. The holidays are always fun here. Easter treats include bunny cakes, which are carrot cakes filled with cream cheese frosting, and decorated with fondant bunny ears.

Whether you're a tourist sauntering by, or you've lived in Plymouth for a lifetime, stop by for a chocolate caramel tart and maybe a shortbread cookie to go. You'll enjoy everything this special shop has to offer.

On the wall in Guilty is a sign that reads, "Wedding—All you need is love and a really fabulous cake." Locals and tourists alike, all we need is the really fabulous Guilty Bakery.

Guilty Bakery

65 Main Street, Plymouth, MA 02360

Hours: Tues & Wed, 10:00AM–4:00PM
Thurs, Fri, Sat, 10:00AM–5:00PM
Sun, 10:00AM–2:00PM

guiltybakery.com

508-927-4724

GUILTY'S FRUIT & OAT BAR

DIRECTIONS

1. Preheat oven to 350°.

2. In a large bowl, mix together melted butter and brown sugar until combined. Add the rest of the dry ingredients—the coconut, flour, oats, and salt. Mix until wet and crumbly. (If dough seems too wet, add up to ¼ C more flour.)

3. Press ²/₃ of the mixture into the bottom of an 8" × 10" pan (or larger) that has been greased and lined with parchment paper. (If you do not have parchment paper, just be sure to grease the pan well.) Chill for about 20 minutes. Keep remaining mixture at room temperature.

4. After 20 minutes, remove the pan from the refrigerator and spread raspberry jam over the top, going all the way to the edges. Sprinkle frozen fruit over the top of the jam layer (use your preference on the amount).

5. Take remaining oat mixture and crumble on the top of the frozen berries. Bake at 350° for about 20–30 minutes or until top is light brown and fruit is bubbly.

6. Let rest at room temperature for about an hour, then chill for another hour. This makes for an easier removal from the pan. Cut into squares and enjoy! Bars can be kept in a covered container on the counter, for about 4 days.

This recipe yields about 20 bars. This is one of our most popular bars in the bakery. We hope it becomes one of yours as well!

INGREDIENTS

1 lb unsalted butter, melted

2 C brown sugar

1 C shredded coconut

2½ C all-purpose flour

2½ C old-fashioned oats

1 tsp salt

1 C raspberry jam

1–2 C frozen fruit (mixed berries and cranberries are the favorite at Guilty Bakery)

Hearth Artisan Bread

The moment you walk into Hearth Artisan Bread, you realize that this is not some kind of fancy, frilly, shi-shi bakery. This is a place where *real* bread is made from precious ingredients, in state-of-the-art hearth ovens imported from Europe, a daily labor of love. And then you see in the variety, from rustic rosemary to ciabatta, that this is more like an artist's studio. Great, edible art is created here.

Peter Nyberg and his wife, Nicole Fichter Nyberg, started Hearth Artisan Bread in 2010. They believe that fine bread should be available to all, and they wanted to return to the simple, delicious breads of old. After working in five-star restaurants, Peter Nyberg, a professionally trained chef with a French culinary degree, decided he wanted to focus on bread.

Peter created the recipes over the past 26 years and uses only healthy, unprocessed ingredients. This traditional, natural leavened bread is a slow process, made in small batches—and you can taste the care they put into each creation. When Peter puts the bread in the oven, he knows which of his bakers mixed and shaped each loaf. "You have to nurture the bread," he told me. His attention to the process seems like a higher calling. When you walk through the door, the scent is heavenly. Bread is stacked on racks to be taken to the best restaurants and hotels on the South Shore and Boston. And some waits on shelves to be bought by lucky, loyal, locals. Kids love the sourdough and learn quickly that this is what real bread is supposed to taste like, developing a life-long healthy habit.

The French country bread is a classic and may just be the best bread you've ever tasted. People come from all over for the six-braid challah and no weekend is complete without a loaf of cinnamon raisin or the elegant cranberry orange candied ginger. Hearth generously gave us the recipe for Cardamom & Golden Raisin Loaf, which happens to be wonderful with strawberry jam. Bread remains a much-loved staple of cuisines all over the world. The beauty of good bread is alive and baking at Hearth Artisan Bread.

Hearth Artisan Bread

123 Camelot Drive, Plymouth, MA 02360

Hours: Daily, 8:00AM–6:00PM

hearthartisanbread.com

774-773-9388

CARDAMOM & GOLDEN RAISIN LOAF

This bread is something I make for my daughters on weekends—one of the best smells they remember growing up. We use it for toast with homemade jams or for French toast. The process that is quick and easy. It can be made Friday afternoon and be out of the oven by early evening.

— Nicole Fichter Nyberg

DIRECTIONS

1. In a mixer equipped with a dough hook, combine the first six ingredients. First, turn on the mixer to low speed and mix the ingredients for 3 minutes. Then lower the mixer and scrape the sides to ensure all ingredients are being incorporated. Continue on low speed for 3 more minutes.

2. Increase the mixing speed to medium-high for 5 minutes. After 2 minutes, start adding the 12 tablespoons of butter little by little, incorporating all the butter within 1 minute. Continue mixing for the 3 remaining minutes.

3. After the butter is fully incorporated, lower the mixing bowl. Add the raisins, and mix on low speed for about 1 minute.

4. Remove dough from mixer and place in a lightly greased bowl to proof. Cover with plastic wrap and allow to rise in a warm place for about 1 hour. Unwrap the bowl and pull up each corner of the dough into the center, then flip the dough over. Cover the bowl with plastic wrap again and allow to proof for another 50 minutes.

5. Spray the 2 pans with non-stick spray. Flour your surface and divide dough into 2 equal pieces. Flatten out each into a rectangle and roll up from one end to the other, then drop the loaf into the pan.

6. Allow the loaves to proof in the pans (covered with plastic wrap) for 50–60 minutes. Once the loaves are about ½ inch from the top of the loaf pan, it's time to bake.

7. Preheat oven to 375°. Place the loaves in the middle part of your oven, and bake for 40–45 minutes.

8. Remove the pans from the oven, carefully unmold and allow to cool on a wire cooling rack. Cool for a few hours before slicing.

INGREDIENTS

2 C whole milk (at room temp)

2½ tsp instant yeast

5 C bread flour

2 tsp sugar

1½ tsp salt

2 tsp ground cardamom

12 T butter (softened)

½ C golden raisins

You will also need:

2 bread loaf pans (8½" × 4½" × 2½")

KitchenAid®-style automatic mixer with dough hook

mixing bowl

plastic wrap

Isaac's Restaurant

Plymouth is a town with a deep respect for history. It's a place where time is a main character, where stories and endurance are important and synonymous. Isaac's opened its doors in 1990 and has flourished in this town where only quality lasts. Isaac's is where you went after graduation, or for your anniversary, or birthday. Whether you visit Isaac's to celebrate with family, enjoy a romantic dinner, or even a business lunch, it's a jewel passed down through the decades for locals and tourists alike.

Isaac Allerton was one of the original and more colorful of Plymouth's original settlers. He had a head for business and was the first assistant governor of the colony. Governor Bradford sent Isaac Allerton back to England a number of times to raise capital and represent the colony to the crown. Were he here now, he would love the panoramic view of the pristine harbor and distant sea through the huge dining room windows. This may truly be the view that you've been dreaming about.

When you rise to the top floor on the elevator you immediately sense that this restaurant is as classic as its perfect vantage point. The menu portrays that attitude in its classic dishes and delicious presentations from fresh seafood, Italian favorites, and fine cuts of steak, to the signature dish Veal Saltimbocca that the chef has shared with us here.

The fragrance of fine food fills the air while you gaze out to sea. Surf and turf, char-grilled marinated pork loin, filet mignon, chicken and shrimp apricot, all taste just as good as their aroma. The lunch menu has a great variety of special dishes, soups, chowders, and salads, as well as a large array of sandwiches and burgers.

There is a long elegant bar, an outdoor seating area, and a large function room. Lunch and dinner are served seven days a week. There is a free parking lot for patrons and lots of on-street parking. Isaac's is always well-staffed and service is knowledgeable, prompt, and friendly. Isaac's makes every occasion special.

Isaac's Restaurant

114 Water Street, Plymouth, MA 02360

Hours: Mon–Sat, 11:30AM–10:30PM

Sun, 11:00AM–10:00PM

isaacsdining.com

508-830-0001

VEAL SALTIMBOCCA

DIRECTIONS

1. In a large sauté pan, heat the oil over medium heat.

2. Dredge the veal medallions in flour. Add medallions to the hot sauté pan and cook both sides evenly for a few minutes per side, until lightly browned.

3. Drain off any oil in the pan and turn heat to low.

4. Top the medallions with a layer of thinly sliced of prosciutto, then Swiss cheese.

5. Scoot the medallions to one side of the pan. In the open space, add the butter. When melted, add the flour and whisk for a moment. Add the Marsala wine, and whisk again for a moment.

6. Incorporate the medallions with the sauce so everything is covered evenly. Add the mushrooms, cover, and let simmer for approximately 5 minutes.

Serve over linguini pasta. Garnish with a sprig of parsley or chopped parsley. Serves 2.

INGREDIENTS

1 T extra virgin olive oil

12 oz veal medallions

flour for dredging

thinly sliced proscuitto

thinly sliced Swiss cheese

4 T butter

2 T flour

½ C Marsala wine

1 C sliced mushrooms

6 oz linguini pasta

parsley for garnish

The Jolly Bean Cafe

The Jolly Bean Cafe

88 Camelot Drive, #24,
Plymouth, MA 02360

Hours: Mon–Fri, 7:00AM–3:00PM
Sat, 7:00AM–2:00PM
Closed Sundays

508-747-2326

Perhaps the Jolly Bean Cafe is L-shaped because it stands for *love* or maybe *lively*. This is one of the most welcoming places to eat in Plymouth. It feels like everyone loves working here. The staff goes out of their way to make sure you're enjoying your meal and it's such a happy and bright place to eat. Owner Amanda Roy has created a hidden jewel of a cafe. Hidden because it's located in a surprising part of Plymouth, just behind the popular Grove at Plymouth shopping plaza. Tucked away, at the edge of an industrial park, but really only five minutes tops from downtown Plymouth, it's a treasure well worth finding.

Stop in for one of their yummy breakfast sandwiches and one of the first things you'll notice is the music playing—always something interesting and upbeat. Then you'll notice how amazing a breakfast burrito can taste. Try the Bad Boy—three eggs, cheese, and homemade sausage, bacon, potato hash—hearty and delicious. The PB & Jamie adds peanut butter, jelly, and bacon to an English muffin—a nice surprise, bacon and jelly. The refreshing Healthy Breakfast Salad includes two eggs, sautéed mushrooms, onions, spinach, avocado, and feta cheese over a bed of baby spinach with Asian sesame dressing. So good you'll find yourself craving the taste. There are also gluten-free and vegetarian choices.

The Jolly Bean has created innovative and scrumptious sandwiches and some of the best soups on the South Shore. The roasted broccoli soup is not to be missed, as is their homemade chicken salad sandwich. The choices and the quality of the food and coffee served here are impressive. And there are always surprises! On a recent afternoon they had hot apple cider on hand—a rare treat on a cool, rainy day. There's always a range of sweet treats—recently, mouth-watering lemon-blueberry cookies. The Jolly Bean Cafe is so much more than jolly. It's a delightful eatery you'll be happy to discover.

HEALTHY BREAKFAST SALAD

DIRECTIONS

1. Sauté the mushrooms and onions for a few minutes. Add one big handful of spinach to the pan, and cook just long enough for it to wilt. Take pan off heat and set aside.

2. Fry the 2 eggs to your liking, and set aside.

3. Meanwhile, put the remaining handful of uncooked spinach in a shallow serving bowl or plate.

4. To your bowl with the uncooked spinach, add the sautéed veggies, fried eggs, sliced avocado, and feta cheese. Season with salt and pepper to your liking.

5. Add all the dressing ingredients to a mixing bowl and whisk well. Drizzle with dressing and enjoy!

FOODIE FACT

Did you know avocado can be used to soothe sunburned skin? Just mash up half a ripe avocado and mix with 1 T olive oil or aloe gel. Use directly on sunburned skin. You can even use this as a facial mask, or in your hair as a deep conditioner. Just leave on for 15 minutes, then rinse off.

INGREDIENTS

¼ C mushrooms, sliced

¼ C yellow onions, sliced

2 big handfuls of baby spinach

2 eggs

half a ripe avocado, sliced

2 oz feta cheese, crumbled

salt and pepper, to taste

ASIAN DRESSING:

¼ cup soy sauce

1 T orange juice

2 T sesame oil

$1/3$ C rice wine vinegar

¼ C extra virgin olive oil

1½ T honey

KKatie's Burger Bar

KKatie's Burger Bar (pronounced Kuh-Katies) opened in 2010, bringing burger bliss to Plymouth. Locals say the burgers here are perfection. They are always fresh, 100% Angus beef, thick and slow-cooked on a flat-top grill. Owner Kate McSorley told me that's what makes all the difference. "When the meat is cooked on a flat-top, there's lots of flavor on that grill, all the juices stay in—all the goodness stays in there." They also hand-form the patties every day, all things Kate's father taught her. And these half-pound burgers are the most creative burgers you've ever tasted.

Sink your teeth into their juicy Peppercorn Steak Burger—a peppercorn-encrusted burger, topped with bleu cheese and caramelized onions, lettuce, tomato, crispy cherry-wood smoked bacon, and KKatie's shallot/garlic mayo on a grilled onion brioche bun. You may never bring yourself to order anything else. Or how about the barbeque burger—topped with cheddar-Jack cheese, crispy cherry-wood smoked bacon, crunchy onion rings, covered in a smoky/sweet barbeque sauce, and served on a grilled sesame seed bun. KKatie's is a *South Shore Living Magazine's* "Best Burger" winner, voted best on the South Shore to Cape Cod for the past four years!

Even the sides are special here—sweet potato fries, the wildly addictive tater tots, freshly made potato chips, and their amazing green bean fries. Make sure you start with some of their renowned appetizers— the fresh, fried mozzarella wedges are so good you'll never order them anywhere else, and the teriyaki chicken pot stickers are served with your choice of spicy sweet red chili sauce or teriyaki sauce. Great salads and sandwiches are also available. And don't forget the specialty drinks, like the Hotel California tequila blood orange margarita. Finish with a Cakke Kkup—dark chocolate devil's food cake, vanilla ice cream, chocolate sauce, and whipped cream, served in a mug.

KKatie's Burger Bar excels at all the details, fresh high-quality Angus beef, innovative sauces and toppings, melt-in-your-mouth buns, and a friendly and expert waitstaff. Your burger is waiting for you at KKatie's, and it's a burger you'll love.

KKatie's Burger Bar

38 Main Street Ext, Plymouth, MA 02360

Hours: Daily, 11:30AM–1:00AM

kkaties.com

774-773-9444

KKatie's Peppercorn Steak Burger

INGREDIENTS

CARAMELIZED ONIONS:
1 T olive oil
1 T butter
1 lb (3 large) yellow onions, sliced thin
1 tsp sugar
1 T balsamic vinegar
¼ tsp kosher salt
$^1/_8$ tsp freshly ground black pepper

SHALLOT/GARLIC MAYO:
6 peeled shallots
6 peeled garlic cloves
1 tsp olive oil
1 tsp sugar
kosher salt to taste
freshly ground pepper to taste
1 C mayo
1 C sour cream
1 tsp Worcestershire sauce

BURGER:
8 oz fresh hamburger patty
2 tsp freshly crushed peppercorns
2 oz caramelized onions (see recipe)
2 oz bleu cheese crumbles
1 tsp soft butter
1 onion brioche bun
2 slices crisp, cooked smoked bacon
1 crisp romaine lettuce leaf
1 slice beefsteak tomato
1 oz shallot/garlic mayo (see recipe)

DIRECTIONS

1. **First, make the caramelized onions.** Heat olive oil in a large skillet (with lid) over med-high heat, add butter to melt. Add onions and pinch of salt, stir then reduce heat to med-low. Cover and cook for 15–20 minutes, stirring occasionally.
2. Remove lid, add sugar, and continue to cook over med-low heat for 10–15 minutes, until golden, stirring frequently to scrape up any browned bits.
3. Add balsamic vinegar, and stir until liquid evaporates, about 1 minute.
4. Season with salt and pepper, to taste, then set aside.
5. **Next, make the shallot/garlic mayo.** Place shallots and garlic in roasting pan. Toss with olive oil and sugar. Sprinkle with salt and pepper. Cover pan with lid or foil and roast in oven at 375° for approximately 40–50 minutes, or until garlic and shallots are soft. Check at halfway point.
6. When cooled, puree garlic and shallots in food processor until almost smooth. Add remaining ingredients, pulse until blended. Set aside.
7. **Finally, make the burger.** Pat the meat lightly with your open palms to form a 5-inch patty. TIP: Do not over handle it or it will become tough.
8. Lightly salt the burger. Put the peppercorns on small plate and press burger into the peppercorns to coat. Repeat on the other side.
9. Heat a cast iron skillet (or heavy skillet) for 2 minutes on med-high heat. Lightly coat the pan with oil. Put patty in skillet and cook for about 5 minutes, until bottom of burger has formed a brown peppercorn crust. Do not press or move the burger. Then flip, and cook other side another 4–5 minutes for medium rare, or 7 minutes for medium.
10. In the pan, place caramelized onions on burger, then bleu cheese. Add one teaspoon of water to pan and cover with lid to melt, about 10–15 seconds. This needs to be done quickly so you don't ruin the burger's crust.
11. Spread butter on inside of bun and grill in a separate pan until golden.
12. Place burger on bottom half of bun, top with bacon, then lettuce and tomato. Spread garlic shallot mayo on top half of bun. Enjoy!

Kogi Korean BBQ

Kogi Korean BBQ & Lounge is a stylish mixture of the old and the new. Delicious food cooked from centuries-old recipes served in a contemporary, beautifully designed dining room and lounge. The restaurant is family owned and operated by husband and wife team Patti Cho and Thuyet Phan, and Patti's mom cooks and helps as well.

Kogi (pronounced Coe-Gi) means any type of meat, and *Korean BBQ* refers to the method of grilling beef, pork, chicken, or other proteins. This restaurant elevates the preparation of meat to an art form. From the list of appealing appetizers such as chicken or pork gyoza (dumplings), chicken skewers, or asparagus tempura to traditional Korean entrees—a must-try is the mouth-watering bibimbap, a sizzling, crispy-crusted rice bowl topped with carrots, mushrooms, spinach, zucchini, bean sprouts, and onions, accompanied with Korean hot sauce and an over easy egg. Add beef or tofu for even more deliciousness. The Kimchi Bokkeum Bap—fried rice made with kimchi—is delectable and healthy. Around the world, chefs are adding kimchi to their dishes for all the health benefits attributed to this fermented cabbage dish. Accompany this with an Asian special bubble tea—lychee or plum with strawberry bubbles is light and sweet. Add rum or vodka to the tea at cocktail hour.

There is so much to enjoy at Kogi, fans come from all over for the fresh sushi and it's a pleasure to eat in the lovely and serene dining area. The elegant bar is also a sought after meeting place with so many choices for drinks. You'll want to relax with raspberry sake or become one of the aficionados who enjoy the extensive Kogi whiskey list, one of the largest in Plymouth. Perhaps a Deveron 12-year single-malt scotch or an Old Potrero single-malt straight rye whiskey. They have so much here to sample.

From the authentic Korean dishes to the elegant and graceful atmosphere, Kogi Korean BBQ & Lounge will become one of your favorites.

Kogi Korean BBQ & Lounge

8 Court Street, Plymouth, MA 02360

Hours: Tue–Sun, 12:00–9:00PM

Closed Mondays

kogikoreanbbq.com

508-927-4105

KIMCHI BOKKEUM BAP

DIRECTIONS

1. Cook rice according to package directions, then set aside.
2. Chop the kimchi, then set aside.
3. Dice the onions, then set aside.
4. Add the oil to your pan and heat over medium. If you are using meat, add your pork or beef and cook thoroughly.
5. When pork or beef is fully cooked, remove from pan and set aside.
6. To the hot pan, now add the onions and kimchi and cook for 5 minutes over medium heat.
7. Add minced garlic and scallions and turn heat to low.
8. Add in the cooked rice and mix ingredients thoroughly.
9. Add sesame oil, kimchi juice, and soy sauce and turn up heat to medium.
10. In a separate pan, cook the eggs sunny-side-up. (Optionally, you may beat the eggs and add directly into the fried rice, stirring until cooked.)
11. Turn off heat and place fried rice onto a dish, then top with your pork or beef, then the egg, and garnish with crumbled nori.

Serves 2.

FOODIE FACT

Kimchi, a fermented cabbage dish, is an ancient staple in Korean cuisine, and a national dish of both South and North Korea. The practice of Kimjang, the autumn tradition of making and sharing kimchi, reaffirms Korean identity and strengthens family bonds and cooperation. Kimjang is also an important reminder for many Koreans that human communities need to live in harmony with nature. Kimchi for peace!

INGREDIENTS

2 C short-grain rice

1 C kimchi, chopped

½ C onion, diced

3 T of canola (or preferred) oil

1 C sliced pork or beef (optional)

1 tsp fresh garlic, minced

2 T fresh scallions, minced

1 tsp sesame oil

2 T kimchi juice

2 T soy sauce

2 eggs

1 pinch of salt

nori sheet (roasted seaweed) for garnish

Leena's Kitchen

Leena grew up in Italy, raised in a tradition of cooking as an expression of love. She made everything by hand and from scratch with ingredients from the garden and recipes passed down through generations. It's fitting that her grandchildren would celebrate her love and respect for food by naming their restaurant Leena's Kitchen. Every meal served here is prepared to be the very best meal you've ever tasted.

Plymouth is a melting pot where many cultures have come together to live and thrive. The Italians are a big part of Plymouth history. Here is a restaurant that all Italians can be proud of and feel that old-world love of food in a contemporary American environment. From the long elegant bar to the cozy private seating, Leena's shines with a smooth, modern feel. Contemporary Italy resides on Long Pond Road, hidden away like a tasty, fragrant feast.

Daniel Casinelli with his sister, Lisa Marsh, and chef extraordinaire, Christopher Collins, have created Leena's wonderful, ever-changing menu, its style, and its high standard of excellence. The service is friendly, knowledgeable, and attentive without being intrusive. Your needs are anticipated and attended to.

The food is sheer perfection. There are incredible salads, fresh and complex, with an amazing assortment of authentic Italian cheeses and meats. The appetizers include fried lobster ravioli with honey truffle aioli, sautéed mussels and littlenecks, arancini, braised short rib, and oysters on the half shell, just to name a few.

Dinners include braised lamb shank, pork Milanese, grilled swordfish, filet mignon, wild boar Bolognese, and always new additions. There are also tasting portions and dollar appetizers daily (except Saturday) from 4:30 to 6:00PM. The elegant desserts include the amazing Bread Pudding featured here. Leena's hosts parties and functions of all kinds for groups of up to 70 guests, and monthly wine dinners. In fall 2018, the group opened SALT, Raw Bar + Fine Cuisine, on the Plymouth waterfront. Plymouth food-lovers are thrilled over this new edition as well!

Leena's Kitchen

63 Long Pond Road, Plymouth, MA 02360

Hours: Tue–Thur & Sun, 4:30PM–9:30PM;
Fri & Sat, 4:30PM–10:30PM

leenaskitchen.com

774-404-7470

BREAD PUDDING

DIRECTIONS

1. Cut crust off all sides of the brioche loaf. Cut brioche into 1-inch cubes. Lightly toast the cubes on a cooking sheet at 350° for approximately 3–5 minutes.

2. In a large bowl, whisk 1 cup of the sugar and egg yolks until completely combined.

3. In a 6-quart pot, heat the heavy cream, the remaining 1 cup of sugar, and the vanilla extract until cream begins to simmer and rise.

4. Temper egg and sugar mixture by slowly adding the hot cream to the eggs. You do not want the eggs to cook, so add the cream slowly. Whisk eggs and cream vigorously while combining.

5. Fold in the toasted brioche cubes to your mixing bowl using a rubber spatula. Be careful not to break the bread apart too much.

6. Fold in fruit of your choice.

7. Pour all ingredients into a greased 13" × 9" baking pan. Cover pan with tin foil and bake at 325° for 30–35 minutes. Allow bread pudding to completely cool before cutting and serving.

This is excellent paired with vanilla ice cream. Serves about 6.

INGREDIENTS

1 large loaf brioche bread

2 C granulated sugar

6 egg yolks

6 C heavy whipping cream

1 tsp vanilla extract

1 C fruit of choice
(mixed berries work well)

Local Yolk Company

Local Yolk Company is *the* place to go when you want to enjoy a peek at Plymouth Harbor along with your ricotta-lemon pancakes, or maybe sausage, biscuits, and gravy. As you dig into some of the best breakfasts and lunches in Plymouth, you can dine outdoors on the deck and watch fishermen getting ready to set sail. Or, enjoy the cozy inside diner-like ambiance as you marvel at your dish of perfect waffles with blueberries or chocolate chips.

Aptly named, this is a place locals frequent, but it's also an enjoyable café where tourists are welcome. You may even find yourself chatting with a traveler from England or Sweden over your chorizo wrap.

Owner Gabby Dominguez has brought a New England artistry to her table, each simple meal impeccably created and served with pride. Her Crispy Fried Egg Breakfast is a combination of perfectly cooked soft-boiled eggs encased in a delicate crispiness so delectable, you'll want to savor each spoonful. This dish is accompanied by arugula salad and a root vegetable hash made of sweet potatoes, parsnips, and carrots—beautiful and delicious! Everything is made from scratch here, and eggs from Gabby's own chickens are available.

The Mayflower panini with cranberry chutney, and the homemade blackberry and bacon panini are among the treats for lunch. And something the locals know: Ms. Dominguez is an amazing baker. I can't leave this restaurant without taking with me a piece of her apple pie or fresh blueberry muffins. If you're looking for gluten-free, try her gluten-free cookies; you can't tell them from regular. And don't miss her sherry cake, with just a sweet hint of nutmeg, a yummy dessert you may not find anywhere else.

Local Yolk Company is a treasure of seaside comfort food, friendly servers, and memorable meals.

Local Yolk Company

186 Water Street, Plymouth, MA 02360
Hours: Daily, 6:00AM–2:00PM
localyolkcompany.com
508-747-4141

CRISPY FRIED EGG BREAKFAST

DIRECTIONS—FOR ROOT VEGGIE HOME FRIES

1. Bring 4 cups of water to a boil. While you are waiting for the water to boil, peel and chop the root vegetables into ½-inch cubes.

2. Lightly salt the water and add the vegetables. Simmer for 10 minutes or until soft. Drain and set aside.

3. Heat the oil in a large cast iron pan over medium-high heat. (The Local Yolk likes EVOO, but make sure the area is under a fan, as it may create smoke. Otherwise, use canola or vegetable oil.)

4. Add the drained vegetables to the hot pan. Turn the vegetables occasionally, but keep in mind that the more you turn them, the harder it will be to get them good and crispy.

5. Add seasonings and adjust to taste. Stir a few more minutes, then remove from heat.

DIRECTIONS—FOR CRISPY EGGS

1. First, set up your breading station: one bowl with the flour, one with the beaten eggs, and one with the panko bread crumbs. The Local Yolk recommends adding salt and pepper to the flour to help flavor the fried coating.

2. Bring 4 cups of heavily salted water to a boil. Use a pot with a tight lid, as the extra pressure will help the eggs cook evenly. Add the 2 eggs to the boiling water, cover, and simmer for exactly 5 minutes.

3. Remove eggs from water with a slotted spoon and place in a bowl of ice water. Allow eggs to cool in the water for a few minutes. Then gently tap the eggs and start removing the shells.

4. Gently dry the eggs with a paper towel. Then gently coat each egg with first the flour, then the beaten eggs, then the panko crumbs.

5. After your oil is heated to temp for deep frying, fry the eggs just a few minutes, until golden brown.

6. Plate your eggs, and salt and pepper to taste. Plate your root vegetable home fries, along with a small salad of arugula, grape tomatoes, and balsamic dressing. Enjoy!

INGREDIENTS

ROOT VEGGIES:
- 1 carrot
- 1 sweet potato
- 1 parsnip
- 1 onion

3T oil of choice

SEASONINGS:
- 1 tsp onion powder
- 1 tsp garlic power
- 1 tsp paprika
- salt, to taste
- pepper, to taste

1 C flour

2 eggs, beaten

2 eggs for soft boiling

1 C panko bread crumbs

oil for deep frying

arugula

grape tomatoes

balsamic dressing

Main Street Sports

Dine and hang out where everybody knows your name. The Main Street Sports Bar & Grill is a fun and friendly place where you can relax at the bar and watch your favorite teams play on the many big screens.

Beer selections include local favorites, and the Grill's Pitcher and Pizza special for $9.99 runs seven days a week—a real fan pleaser! There are always great deals here at Main Street Sports. Don't miss the $5 sandwiches on Tuesdays. And for entertainment there are trivia nights, and live music every night! The Main Street Sports Bar & Grill is a wonderful supporter of local music.

In the summer, the windows of the Grill open on to Main Street in Plymouth and you can watch the crowds saunter by, while enjoying Italian quesadillas or a basket of sweet onion rings. The Grill has great appetizers and is family friendly. On a recent evening, I nibbled a Caesar salad from a comfortable window seat as a dad and his son watched a Celtics game over cheeseburgers and sweet potato fries.

One favorite here is Chef Sean Chumley's amazing Ranch Dressing, which is the perfect accompaniment for everything—from a heaping plate of chicken tenders to juicy BBQ-marinated steak tips. Chef Chumley has been working in kitchens since he was 18 and his experience shows in the quality of food he serves. While trying to decide what to do with his life, he fell in love with cooking. At an early age, he was reading cookbooks from beginning to end, the way other young kids read comics.

In Massachusetts, we do love our Red Sox and Patriots, and there is something wonderful about enjoying an ice-cold pitcher of beer in a quintessential sports bar. Here in New England, we take our sports seriously and it doesn't get any better than this restaurant for a fan. Fan tip: Don't miss the spicy linguiça clam chowder. And during the baseball playoffs, don't miss the Main Street Sports Bar & Grill—a New England classic. Cheers!

Main Street Sports Bar & Grill

39 Main Street, Plymouth, MA 02360

Hours: Daily, 11:00AM–1:00AM

mainstreetsportsbarandgrill.com

774-283-4129

RANCH DRESSING & DRY RUB

DIRECTIONS & INGREDIENTS

For the Ranch Dressing, mix well the following ingredients. Refrigerate and use as needed.
Yields 1½ cups.

- 1 C mayonnaise
- ½ C sour cream
- 1½ tsp dried parsley
- 1½ tsp dried dill
- 1½ tsp dried chives
- ¾ tsp granulated garlic
- ¾ tsp granulated onion
- ½ tsp kosher salt
- ½ tsp black pepper
- 1 T buttermilk

For the Ranch Dry Rub, mix well the following ingredients. This is a great flavor enhancer for chicken wings, or just about any kind of meat. Also try it sprinkled over veggies or even a baked potato. It's very versatile!
Yields 1¼ cups.

- ¼ C dried chives
- ¼ C dried dill
- ¼ C dried parsley
- 2 T granulated garlic
- 2 T granulated onion
- 2 T kosher salt
- 2 T ground black pepper

Martini's Bar & Grill

Walk through the heart of downtown and you'll find one of Plymouth's most charming restaurants for both delicious food and exciting live music. Martini's is a perfect mixture of elegance and wonderful cuisine. Sitting in the stylish dining room brings to mind the sophistication of a Manhattan supper club. From the 1920s to the 1960s, New York City's best supper clubs hosted singers like Ella Fitzgerald and Sarah Vaughan. Picture Marilyn Monroe sipping champagne by candlelight while listening to Frank Sinatra croon and you can feel the ambiance of that era. Today, if you crave a great steak, a classy cocktail, and some cool music, Martini's is the place to go.

Joe Perette and Dave Gervasi share extensive experience in the restaurant business. Dave was executive chef at the Union Chowder House in Weymouth for over 15 years and he has created an inspired menu with everything from fresh seafood to pasta specialties. Start with an appetizer of pumpkin raviolis with sage brown butter, Parmesan, cranberries, and toasted sunflower seeds to delight your taste buds. David's Autumn Scallop Salad with pan-seared scallops, baby arugula, local cranberries, chèvre, roasted pumpkins seeds, and granola with orange cranberry dressing is also a perfect beginning.

Special entrees include the popular filet mignon—certified Black Angus, seasoned and grilled, with a red wine, mushroom demi-glaze. Don't miss the candied pecan salmon—grilled and brushed with house honey-mustard sauce and finished with crushed pecans, along with confetti rice. And whether you're meeting friends at the bar or relaxing over a fine meal, you'll want to have one of their innovative cocktails in hand.

Martini's has quite a menu for the musical palate, with live music from Thursday to Saturday and fabulous jazz by the Kenny Wenzel Trio on Tuesday nights. Kenny's seasoned players sizzle and soar through jazz standards, often joined by great singers like Loretta LaRoche and, until recently, the late Rebecca Paris. In the summer, sit by the open windows, and enjoy all this delightful restaurant has to offer—lunch, dinner, Sunday brunch, and smooth jazz—Martini's serves it all.

Martini's Bar & Grill

50 Court Street, Plymouth, MA 02360
Hours: Mon–Sat, 12:00PM–12:00AM
Sun, 2:00PM–11:00PM
martinisplymouth.com
774-773-9782

AUTUMN SCALLOP SALAD

DIRECTIONS

1. Toss the granola mix of oats, currants, and maple syrup. Place in an even layer on a baking sheet, and bake at 300° for 40 minutes or until crunchy and golden. Remove from oven and set aside.

2. Place the pumpkin seeds on a baking tray and lightly salt. Roast the seeds at 350° for 10–15 minutes, until slightly golden. Watch that they do not burn. Remove from oven and set aside.

3. Make the vinaigrette by combining all dressing ingredients (except the oil, salt, and pepper) into a blender. Blend on high, until well mixed, then drizzle in the oil while continuing to blend. Turn off blender, and add salt and pepper to your liking. Set aside.

4. Next, sear the scallops. NOTE: It's important to use dry-packed scallops, if you are able, to get a good sear. So be sure to ask your grocer or seafood market for dry-packed as opposed to wet-packed scallops. If you can't find dry sea scallops, the wet ones need to be rinsed and dried well to achieve a nice sear.

   a. Rinse the scallops well. If necessary, remove the small tough muscle on the side that may still be attached. Pat them very dry with a paper towel. Season with kosher salt.

   b. In a non-stick skillet, heat oil on medium-high until just about smoking, then add the scallops but don't crowd. Be careful not to move the scallops around. Let them get a good sear, 2 to 3 minutes for large scallops, then gently turn over for 1 minute on the other side.

   c. Add a pat of cold butter at the last 10 seconds to give a nice golden look.

5. Finally, assemble your salads in two bowls. Use baby arugula (or your favorite mixed greens) on the bottom. Top with the chèvre, sprinkle with the roasted pumpkin seeds and granola to your liking, and fresh cranberries. Top with 5 scallops in each bowl, then drizzle with the cranberry vinaigrette.

Serves 2.

INGREDIENTS

GRANOLA MIX:

¼ C oats

¼ C dried currants

½ C maple syrup

---

raw pumpkin seeds

10 large sea scallops

kosher salt

2 T oil

pat cold butter

12 oz baby arugula or mixed greens

½ C fresh cranberries

1 T crumbled chèvre (goat cheese)

CRANBERRY VINAIGRETTE:

2 C orange juice

1 tsp Dijon mustard

splash of sherry wine vinegar

½ C sugar

kosher salt

2 C fresh cranberries

½ C extra virgin olive oil

salt and pepper, to taste

OFFICIAL PLYMOUTH 400 SIGNATURE EVENTS AND PROGRAMS

Plymouth 400, Inc. is planning **Signature Events and Programs** to honor this historic anniversary on a global scale. Each of Plymouth 400's commemorative events and programs highlight America's story of *exploration, innovation, self-governance, religious expression, immigration and thanksgiving.* These legacies, sparked by these historic events, continue today as cornerstones of our nation.

PLYMOUTH 400™
1620-2020

PLYMOUTH 400 COMMEMORATION OPENING CEREMONY
An International Event | April 24, 2020
Location: Memorial Hall and surrounding area, Plymouth, MA

The ceremony will be a cross-cultural spectacle of historical content, visual and performing arts and more. Honoring the past and celebrating the future, each of the commemoration's themes will be presented in creative ways. VIP invitations include national leaders, heads of state, and other international dignitaries.

OFFICIAL MARITIME SALUTE
June 27-28, 2020
Location: Plymouth, MA, Harbor & Waterfront

This event will honor the Pilgrim's Mayflower journey with a parade of sail in and around Plymouth Harbor. A regatta of wooden ships, official vessels, work boats and pleasure craft will culminate in a traditional New England lobster dinner at the waterfront. *Mayflower II* will be a centerpiece of this event.

WAMPANOAG ANCESTORS WALK
August 15, 2020
Location: Plymouth, MA

The Wampanoag Ancestors Walk will be led by people from the Wampanoag tribes of Massachusetts. Placards will be carried with the names of the original 69 villages of the Wampanoag Nation. Participants will pay homage to Massasoit and King Phillip and stop at designated sites to bless the spots where their ancestors once walked. The event will conclude with a drum ceremony and reception.

OFFICIAL STATE HOUSE SALUTE TO THE 400TH ANNIVERSARY
September 14, 2020
Location: Massachusetts State House, Boston, MA

This Ceremony will honor the Pilgrim forefathers and Native people who are immortalized in the historic founding of Plymouth Colony. The rarely seen journal of Governor William Bradford will be on display and State legislators, the governor and other national and international dignitaries will be invited to speak.

EMBARKATION FESTIVAL
A Multi-Day Cultural Festival | September 19 & 20, 2020
Location: Plymouth, MA

This grand cultural and arts festival will honor the traditions, cuisine, and music of not only the original settlers and Wampanoag people but the diverse immigrants who followed and contributed to the fabric of American life. Invited dignitaries will include heads of state, celebrities, and students from around the world.

INDIGENOUS HISTORY CONFERENCE & POWWOW
October 30-November 1, 2020
Location: Bridgewater State University, Bridgewater, MA

The conference will celebrate the longevity and continuity of America's indigenous people. This cultural event will feature the historical and contemporary contributions of the Wampanoag and other Native nations, culminating in a traditional Powwow.

2020 THANKSGIVING EVENTS
Concerts: Nov 20
Parade: Nov 21
"One Small Candle" Ceremony: Nov 22
Thanksgiving Festival Events: Nov 23-24
Illuminate Thanksgiving: Nov 25
Location: Plymouth, MA

This series of events leading up to the Thanksgiving holiday, promotes gratitude and giving. Based upon Governor Bradford's quote, "Just as one small candle may light a thousand, so the light here kindled hath shone unto many…" the One Small Candle Award is given to an individual who has positively affected many.

"OUR"STORY: 400 YEARS OF WAMPANOAG HISTORY
Regional Traveling Exhibit - Ongoing

Told from the Native perspective, "Our"Story is an educational exhibition created to highlight critical elements of Wampanoag history. This exhibition, created by a Wampanoag research and design team, travels regionally. The exhibit expands each year leading up to 2020 with new "chapters" in the history and culture of the "people of the dawn."

www.Plymouth400inc.org

PLYMOUTH 400, INC. | 6 MAIN STREET EXT., PLYMOUTH, MA 02360 | 508.812.2020 | INFO@PLYMOUTH400INC.ORG

The Bistro
& Wine Bar

Open daily for breakfast, lunch & dinner

Located within Mirbeau Inn & Spa at The Pinehills, The Bistro & Wine Bar offers casually elegant dining in a world-class locale. Our seasonal menus include classic French bistro dishes infused with New England flavors, and our extensive wine list offers sophisticated pairings for every dish.

plymouth.mirbeau.com | 877-MIRBEAU | 35 Landmark Drive, Plymouth

Mirbeau Bistro & Wine Bar

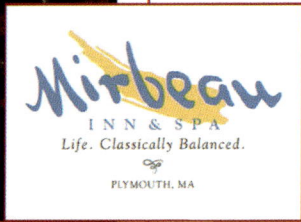

Mirbeau is French for "reflected beauty," and fittingly, the Inn wraps around a water garden with exquisite water lilies and a colorful wooden bridge Monet himself would enjoy painting. Stay the night in the elegant Inn, be pampered in the state-of-the-art spa, and come for the French-inspired menu, infused with local New England flavors. Whether you come for a decadent dinner or a special event, whenever you arrive at this exquisite resort, built in the style of a French château, it's like returning to a dream.

Diners will enjoy the Bistro & Wine Bar, the perfect place for a healthy breakfast. The simple Mirbeau Spa scramble is a satisfying combination of egg whites, tofu, spinach, and oyster mushrooms. The delightful chocolate crêpes feature fresh berries and toasted hazelnuts. Lunch choices highlight delicious salads and soups. The French onion soup is flavorful perfection. The ham and Gruyère quiche is wonderful, and the fig flatbread with prosciutto, arugula, bleu cheese, and caramelized onions is so good you'll crave its rich taste. We are thrilled to present the recipe for the Bistro's classic Tuna Niçoise—lightly seared tuna, plated with field greens, fingerling potatoes, haricot verts, olives, and cherry tomatoes.

Dinner is a range of luscious hors d'oeuvres, popovers, and decadent entrees that include grilled local swordfish, surf and turf, and an excellent potato-crusted salmon with sautéed spinach, lemon beurre, and fingerling potatoes. Don't miss the impressive pappardelle pasta—local lobster, citrus beurre fondue, asparagus, roasted cherry tomatoes, and fresh basil. There is a Sunday jazz brunch, seasonal specialties, and a monthly afternoon tea. An in-house pastry team creates fine desserts like pineapple angel food cake with macerated strawberries, linzer crumble, and toasted pineapple. There is an extensive wine selection and signature cocktails.

The Garden Bar overlooks the ponds and gardens, and features wood-fired pizza with house-made dough and seasonal toppings. Whether you dine at the Bistro & Wine Bar or the cozy Garden Bar, Mirbeau provides everything you need—beauty, relaxation, and delicious food to rival any French country bistro. A beautiful dream made real here in Plymouth.

Mirbeau Bistro & Wine Bar

35 Landmark Drive, Plymouth, MA 02360

Hours: Breakfast daily, 7:00AM–10:00AM
Lunch, Mon–Sat, 11:00AM–4:00PM
Dinner, Sun–Thur 5:00PM–9:00PM
   and Fri & Sat 5:00PM–10:00PM

plymouth.mirbeau.com/dining/bistro

508-209-2393

TUNA NIÇOISE

INGREDIENTS

4 (6 oz) tuna steaks

2 C cooked fingerling potatoes, par cooked until fork soft and cut into moon shapes

2 C haricot verts

2 C cherry tomatoes, cut in halves

2 C mixed olives

¼ C sherry vinaigrette (see step 1 below)

2 sprigs flat leaf parsley, torn by hand into small pieces

2 sprigs tarragon, torn by hand into small pieces

salt and pepper, to taste

SHERRY VINAIGRETTE:

2 oz sherry vinegar

1 T Dijon mustard

1 T honey

1 T shallots, minced

2 oz vegetable oil

2 oz extra virgin olive oil

salt and pepper, to taste

CELERY ROOT PUREE:

1 bulb of celery root, peeled

1T lemon juice

salt and pepper, to taste

NOTE: Serves 4.

DIRECTIONS

1. First, make the sherry vinaigrette. Add the vinegar, mustard, honey, and shallots to a blender. While the motor is running, slowly drizzle in the oils. Add salt and pepper to taste. Remove from blender and set aside.

2. Next, make the celery root puree. Dice the peeled celery root into small pieces and simmer fully submerged in water until completely soft. When soft, strain and add it to a blender. Puree on high until completely pureed. Add lemon juice, season with salt and pepper to taste, and set aside.

3. Next, make the vegetables. Add small amount of vegetable oil to a sauté pan over medium-high heat. When the oil starts to "dance," add potatoes and allow to brown slightly. Add the haricot verts and shake pan until beans become soft. Next, add the tomatoes and olives and cook until everything is hot.

4. Remove from heat. Add vinaigrette. Season with salt and pepper if needed. Add the parsley and tarragon.

5. Place another sauté pan over high heat and add a small amount of oil. Season the tuna with salt and pepper. Sear the tuna in the pan until golden brown on top and bottom, and then remove the steaks from the pan, placing them on a paper towel to absorb excess oil.

6. To plate, drop a heaping tablespoon of the celery root puree onto the left side of each plate, then smear it across the plate with the back of a spoon. Divide the vegetables onto the four plates, placed in the center of each plate. Place the tuna steaks on top of the vegetables.

Piece of Cake

Piece of Cake is a delightful bakery, tucked away on Alden Street in Plymouth, a hidden gem of sweetness. Judy MacPherson started her business in 1986 and it's been growing ever since. Brides all over the South Shore treasure her elegant wedding cakes, and her custom specialty cakes star at events throughout New England. Traditional homemade cake flavors include chocolate, marble, white, yellow, spice, carrot, and the popular half-chocolate/half-vanilla. Topped with exquisite butter cream frosting and filled with lemon, strawberry, Bavarian cream, chocolate, or cherry—just a sampling of choices that create a dessert masterpiece. There are also custom icings of mocha, chocolate, and cream cheese. With all these choices, it's time to start eating dessert first!

Pay a visit to the cake shop and you'll notice the care and beautiful details in every corner. You'll see the gorgeous wedding dress that Judy's mom wore in 1954, then passed along to Judy and Judy's sister for their weddings. Graceful antique chairs and tables, and cupcakes and scones displayed on vintage plates, invite you to sit down and enjoy a cup of coffee and a mixed berry muffin or their special Chocolate Chip Cookies, recipe provided here. You never know what treats Judy and her crew of amazing bakers will whip up. Every day there are special goodies available.

Gluten-free and vegan cupcakes are made to order and you'll find Piece of Cake pastries served in some of the classiest restaurants in Plymouth. Try one of the bakery's fabulous cupcakes. With so many wonderful flavors, it's hard to leave the shop without some. Lemon coconut is a white cake with a lemon curd filling, topped with butter cream and smothered in flaked coconut. The strawberry blonde—gold cake with a strawberry filling, topped with pink butter cream—just might be the prettiest cupcake you've ever seen. Whatever you pick, you'll want to taste the popular triple chocolate cupcake—dark chocolate cake topped with chocolate butter cream and dipped in semi-sweet ganache —a chocolate-lover's dream. Just remember: There's always room for a scrumptious Piece of Cake dessert.

Piece of Cake

34 Alden Street, Plymouth, MA 02360

Hours: Tue–Fri, 10:00AM–6:00PM

Sat, 9:00AM–5:00PM; Sun, 9:00AM–3:00PM

Closed Mondays

508-747-2253

CHOCOLATE CHIP COOKIES

DIRECTIONS

1. Preheat oven to 350°.
2. Mix all ingredients, except the flour and chocolate chips, on slow speed, in a mixer.
3. Slowly add in the sifted flour.
4. Gently fold in the chocolate chips.
5. Bake at 350° for approximately 15–20 minutes, until just starting to turn golden.

FOODIE FACT

If you're from Massachusetts, you likely know that the original chocolate chip cookie was invented at the Toll House Inn in Whitman, Massachusetts in 1938. However, it took decades of national and then worldwide recognition before this melty morsel became the official state cookie of Massachusetts in 1997.

INGREDIENTS

2 large eggs

¾ C light brown sugar

¾ C granulated sugar

1 tsp baking powder

1 tsp salt (optional)

¾ C softened butter

1 tsp vanilla

2¾ C sifted flour

2 C chocolate chips

The Pillory Pub

The approach to the Pillory Pub tells much of its story—laughter, music, conversation, and people. The wooden rockers looking out on Pilgrim Memorial Park are always occupied. What could be more pleasant than sitting in a comfortable rocker with a cold beer or a mixed drink, looking out at the ocean, and rocking the night away?

Inside, the high-tops, tables, and bar are alight with conversation and reverie. There's something about the seating here that facilitates gatherings and friendship. You can sit with your party and if you want, party with the table beside you. There's one big-screen television, which is just the right number. This place is about people, good times, great food, and perfect drinks.

And how many pubs cater to dog lovers—hot dogs that is! These dogs will drive you wild with 13 different styles, snappy tastes, and zesty aromas. There's also a great chicken sandwich, homemade chowder, chili, soups, fresh salads, lobster rolls, and more. The shrimp tacos are a south-of-the-border seafood dish that will tickle your taste buds. We had to spend eight hours in stocks (aka, pilloried) in order to get the Pub Shrimp Tacos recipe shared here, but it was well worth it.

The staff is easy going, professional, and friendly. Owners Ben and Brianna Parsons really make you feel at home. There's good, local live music. And did we mention the long window open to the waterfront and ocean? People watching, dining, sipping on a cool drink, and the feeling that there's nowhere else you have to be. It really is one of those places that you feel comfortable hanging out and just enjoying the company.

The crowd here reflects a variety of Plymouth locals and tourists, mixed together expertly with hospitality, humor, and celebration. You'll hear the laughter as you approach the Pillory Pub, and it will invite you in for a spell. You may not want to leave.

The Pillory Pub

72 Water Street, Plymouth, MA 02360

Hours: Mon–Sat, 11:30AM–12:00AM

Sun, 12:00PM–12:00AM

https://www.facebook.com/The-Pillory-Pub-246995885340566/

774-283-4086

PUB SHRIMP TACOS

INGREDIENTS

a bag of raw, frozen, cleaned shrimp (about 28)

4 C chopped iceberg lettuce

8 flour tortillas

corn chips

BAJA SAUCE:

½ C mayonnaise

½ C sour cream

2 T lime juice

$^1/_8$ C chopped cilantro

1 diced jalapeño, or to taste

1 tsp garlic powder

1 T taco seasoning

SHRIMP TACO SEASONING:

½ T garlic powder

½ T onion powder

1 T taco seasoning

1 T Old Bay® Seasoning

PICO DE GALLO:

4 diced Roma tomatoes

1 diced red onion

2 diced jalapeños

¼ C chopped cilantro

1 tsp salt

1 tsp black pepper

1 tsp garlic powder

2 T lime juice

DIRECTIONS

1. Blend the Baja sauce ingredients in a food processor or blender until smooth. Chill in the refrigerator for at least 1 hour.

2. In a mixing bowl, combine all the pico de gallo ingredients. Chill in the refrigerator for at least 1 hour.

3. In small bowl, mix together the shrimp taco seasoning ingredients. Set aside.

4. Fill a stock pot with water and heat to a boil. Drop the shrimp into the water (about 7 per taco, depending on their size). Boil for a few minutes until done.

5. While the shrimp is boiling, heat the tortillas in a microwave for 20 seconds.

6. Plate the tortillas, 2 per plate. Add a layer of chopped lettuce.

7. Drain shrimp and toss with shrimp taco seasoning. Place seasoned shrimp on top of the lettuce layer. NOTE: You don't need to use all the seasoning if using less shrimp. Just a dusting will do.

8. Top with the fresh pico de gallo and then drizzle with the Baja sauce.

Serve with a side of more pico de gallo and corn tortilla chips for dipping. Serves 4.

Plimoth Plantation

Plimoth Plantation is a living history museum that opened in 1947 with the support of Henry Hornblower II. It is world famous for its continuing studies of the original Plimoth Colony and the native population of the period, along with ongoing preservation, archeology projects, and education. Foodies around the world are also aware of the Plantation's creations of historic culinary delights for lunch, feasts, historically themed dinners, and catered events, such as weddings. The Thanksgiving Day Homestyle Buffet and the Story of Thanksgiving Dinner have been enjoyed by visitors from around the world, and are always booked far in advance.

Groups of 25 or more can enjoy an amazing New England clambake or a sit-down barbecue dinner. Eat Like a Pilgrim is a special group-themed dinner experience. All ages will enjoy a fun and educational experience hosted by a museum educator that will offer them a slice of 17th-century life. Turkey, pompion (squash), sweet Indian corn pudding, cucumber sallet, charger of cheese and fruit, cheate bread, and apple cider. This is a feast fit for a Pilgrim.

A 17th Century Wampanoag Feast includes a sit-down family-style, classic Wampanoag meal featuring fresh seasonal ingredients—turkey, venison stew; nausamp with raspberries, blueberries, and strawberries; squash; three sisters rice; cornbread; dried berries; and mint tea. A Taste of Two Cultures dining experience celebrates the flavors that came from the meeting of two very unique cultures, both of whom loved food. The meal includes a wonderful blending of foods—fricassee of fish, roast fowl with sauce, nausamp, seasonal sallet, summer succotash, Shrewsbury cake, and mint tea. This amazing culinary experience turns into a deeper understanding of two cultures and the 17th century.

The Plantation also serves great box lunches to be enjoyed while exploring the grounds and exhibits, and a café that serves a delightful collection of Pilgrim foods—turkey dinner; Peasecods; Indian pudding; along with sandwiches, soups, and salads. Drinks include Mayflower Beer and assorted coffees and soft drinks. Stop at the Plimoth Plantation for an experience of American history *and* delicious dining.

Plimoth Planation

137 Warren Avenue, Plymouth, MA 02360

Hours: Daily, 9:00AM–5:00PM

plimoth.org

508-746-1622

PEASECODS (SAVORY MEAT PIES)

Peasecods (meaning, shaped like *pea pods*) were 16th century finger-sized meat pies. Cooking savory fillings wrapped within a pie crust was a convenient way to cook and store a food item within its own container.

INGREDIENTS

1 egg yolk for wash

DOUGH:

2¼ C unbleached all-purpose flour

1½ tsp salt

1 stick (½ C) cold unsalted butter, cut into ½-inch slices

1 large egg

$^1/_3$ C ice water

1 T distilled white vinegar

FILLING:

1 lb ground white meat (pork, veal, turkey, or chicken)

½ tsp nutmeg

½ tsp cinnamon

$^1/_8$ tsp ground cloves

¼ tsp ground ginger

½ tsp paprika

½ tsp turmeric

½ tsp salt

¼ tsp black pepper

$^1/_3$ C golden raisins

1 T orange marmalade

1 T softened butter

1 egg yolk

DIRECTIONS

1. In a large bowl, sift together the flour and salt. Blend in butter using a pastry blender or forks until mixture resembles coarse meal (roughly pea-sized lumps).

2. In another bowl, whisk together the egg, water, and vinegar. Add this to the flour mixture, and stir with a fork until just incorporated. It will be a bit sticky.

3. Turn out mixture onto a lightly floured surface and knead gently with heel of your hand once or twice. Form the dough into a ball, then wrap in plastic wrap, and allow to chill for at least 1 hour.

4. While dough is chilling, make your filling. In a bowl, combine the filling ingredients.

5. After dough has chilled, place it onto a lightly floured surface. Roll out the dough to about $^1/_8$-inch thick. Cut into circles with a round cookie cutter or glass.

6. Drop a tablespoon or two of the meat mixture into the center of each dough circle, being careful not to overfill. Fold the dough over the meat and gently squeeze the little peasecods within your hand to make sure they are sealed. They should be small.

7. Place pies on a cookie sheet and brush the tops with beaten egg yolk. Bake at 375° for about 25 minutes, or until golden. These may also be deep fried.

Makes 12–16 pies.

Quahog Republic's Captain's Den

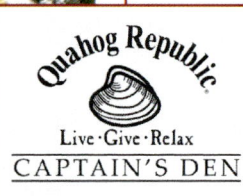

The hottest place in town these days is the Quahog Republic's Captain's Den. Fun events are always happening here: fundraisers, craft beer nights, and just recently a casting call for a movie being filmed in the fall of 2018 (a film adapted from the novel "Running Waves" by T.M. and Seton Murphy). That's the kind of place the Captain's Den is—unassuming on the outside, fun and inventive on the inside.

The comfortable vibe comes from friendly servers and chefs, and traditional food done perfectly. Their quahog chowder is loaded with flavor. Their legendary bloody Marys are made from infused vodka aged in special casks, and pair perfectly with their golden brown stuffed quahog. And their raw bar is overflowing with fresh chilled oysters, shrimp, and littlenecks on the half-shell. Their Crunchy Cod Fish 'n Chips is delicate and delicious with almonds added to the batter. Grab a window table overlooking Main Street, a great people-watching spot and the perfect place to dig into the Den's famous "monsta lobsta roll," available in two sizes. This is one of the best lobster rolls in New England. They delicately clean the meat by hand (no knife touches this lobster!) and then lightly dress the giant chunks of tail and claw, piling it all onto a buttered, toasted brioche bun. Lobsta nirvana!

This Plymouth restaurant is the newest member of the Cape Cod Quahog Republic's group of innovative eating establishments, joining the well-respected New Bedford Whaler's Tavern, Onset's Waterfront Eatery, and Falmouth's Dive Bar. Co-owners Erik Bevans and Tom Hughes are committed to excellence. They take pride in using the highest quality ingredients while paying attention to the details. The ambiance shines here, beautiful exposed brick walls and warm lighting. The owners have a mission: you need to live life to the fullest, give back to the community, and relax. "Live, Give, Relax" became the motto of the Quahog Republic, and they proudly support local charities. I asked Erik Bevans if any celebrities have been in the restaurant, and he quickly said, "All our customers are celebrities to us." At the Captain's Den, they make you feel like family.

Quahog Republic's Captain's Den

35 Main Street, Plymouth, MA 02360

Hours: Food daily, 11:30AM–11:00PM
Bar, Sun–Thur, 11:30AM–Midnight
Bar, Fri & Sat, 11:30AM–1:00AM

quahogrepublic.com/captain-s-den

508-591-7589

CRUNCHY COD FISH 'N CHIPS

DIRECTIONS

1. In a large mixing bowl, whisk all the slaw ingredients together, except the cabbage and carrots, until well blended.

2. To the bowl, add the cabbage and carrots and mix in by hand until evenly incorporated. Your slaw should be a creamy consistency with a tender crunch. Set aside in refrigerator until ready to serve.

3. In a large mixing bowl, add the cream, water, and eggs. Whisk until evenly mixed and pour in to a shallow casserole dish.

4. Next, in another shallow casserole dish, add corn flakes and almonds. Mix them well and crush corn flakes lightly (but do not pulverize).

5. In a third and last casserole dish, add the flour.

6. Take your cod fillets and fully coat with the flour, then the cream and egg mixture, and finally coat the fillets in the corn flake mixture, and then set aside.

7. In a large pot or deep fryer, heat vegetable oil to 350°. Drop your fillets into the oil with a pair of tongs, cook until golden brown. Cooking time will vary depending on the thickness of your fish. Thin fish may require only 2 mintues, and thicker fish 5 minutes or more. Remove from oil to drain on paper towels.

8. When all your fish is cooked and removed from the oil, drop your frozen fries into the oil and cook until golden brown. Remove from oil and salt to taste.

9. Plate with the cod, and the chilled slaw, and some tartar sauce and lemon on the side.

Serves 4.

INGREDIENTS

3 C heavy cream

1 C water

2 eggs

5 C corn flakes

1½ C sliced almonds

2 C flour

4 (6-oz) cod fillets, rinsed and patted dry

1 gal vegetable oil

32 oz frozen French fries

salt, to taste

COLESLAW:

3½ C mayonnaise

1½ C white sugar

$1/3$ C apple cider vinegar

1 tsp salt

¼ C dry mustard

2 T Cajun seasoning

1 T celery salt

1 tsp hot sauce

half a head green cabbage, shredded

1 small carrot, shredded

Rye Tavern

In 1792, Joseph and Abigail Cornish built the Cornish Tavern in what was considered an outlying area and one of two Plymouth stagecoach stops. This beautiful 18th century building is now the Rye Tavern, and though no longer a coach stop, it is still a tavern where you can enjoy comfort in any season along with the finest food and drink.

Situated at the edge of the Pinehills, the Rye Tavern is surrounded by woods, gravel paths and roads, and a huge garden. The garden provides the Rye with flowers, specialty greens, and herbs during the growing season. Some 30 local farmers supply the remaining vegetables and herbs in a true farm-to-table fashion. John Adams, who stayed and ate at the Tavern in 1794, would most likely approve of this wholesome, locally sourced culinary wonder.

The Rye is a dining experience that embraces seasonal beauty. In the warm weather, the outdoor bar and ample outdoor seating area is peaceful and private, surrounded by trees and gardens. In the colder months, a beautiful crackling fire adds to the sounds of laughter and conversation, and along with the natural wood and large beamed ceilings, this truly feels like that old stagecoach stop.

The food at the Rye Tavern is a wonderful mix of superb ingredients, interesting recipes, skillful execution, and a changing seasonal menu. Brunch on Saturday and Sunday is a combination of beautifully prepared breakfast favorites, such as the crab omelet and salmon hash. The lunch menu adds a colorful assortment of sandwiches, wraps, and burgers (of grass-fed beef). About every eight weeks the menu changes, highlighting a new risotto or locally sourced seafood dish. Each visit to the Rye Tavern introduces delightful surprises.

Dinner shines with dishes such as baked vindaloo sausage and gnudis, and pan-seared salmon. The appetizers are wonderfully unique, the salads crisp and original, and the desserts definitely worth saving room for. This season featured fresh peaches and candied cashews atop Chocolate Espresso Cheesecake, a recipe that is unforgettable. The Rye Tavern will offer you a taste of history, along with the finest of contemporary cuisine.

Rye Tavern

517 Old Sandwich Rd., Plymouth, MA 02360

ryetavern.com | 508-591-7515

~ Open 7 days a week ~
Bar opens at 4PM
Dinner service at 5PM
~ Offering ~
Saturday & Sunday brunch 11AM–2PM
Dinner service begins at 5PM

Chocolate Espresso Cheesecake

DIRECTIONS

1. Bring a pot of water to a simmer. Place the chocolate chips in a metal bowl and place the bowl over the water to melt the chocolate chips. Or use a double boiler for this purpose, if you have one. Gently stir the chocolate from time to time, until melted.

2. In a food processer, puree the heavy cream and egg yolks. Cut cream cheese into small cubes and add a few at a time while the processer is running. Then add salt, orange zest and juice, vanilla, sugar, and espresso. Last, add all the melted chocolate.

3. Use pan spray on your baking dish of choice and pour mixture into. This will yield seven 4-oz ramekins (or you may use a glass pie pan to make one large cheesecake).

4. Place your baking dishes in a large, shallow casserole dish, and fill this casserole dish with water so that it comes halfway up your cheesecake baking dishes. This is known as a hot water bath, or bain-marie. Wrap the tops of your cheesecake dishes with foil. Bake at 350° for 20 minutes. Allow to chill and set before serving.

Adorn with your favorite toppings, such as local fresh fruit, whipped cream, or fresh mint.

FOODIE FACT

Placing a baking dish in a hot water bath is a gentle way to cook delicate foods such as custard or cheesecake. In the culinary world, this is known as a bain-marie (pronounced "bane mah-REE"). The purpose of a bain-marie is that it creates a gentle heat around the food and results in a uniform cooking process. If you've ever made a cheesecake that ends up with a big crack down the center when done, a bain-marie may help alleviate this dreaded outcome.

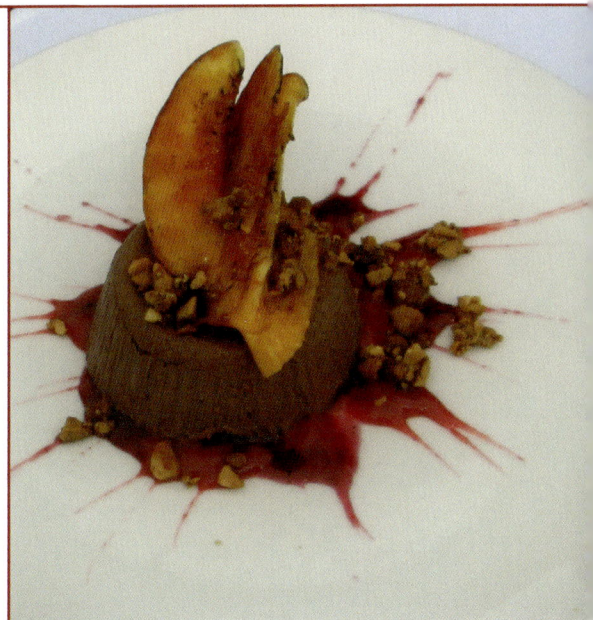

INGREDIENTS

1 C chocolate chips

2 C heavy cream

8 egg yolks

1 lb cream cheese, at room temperature

½ tsp salt

zest and juice from 1 orange

½ tsp vanilla extract

½ C granulated sugar

1 T instant espresso

Second Wind Brewing Co.

With the list of local breweries within Plymouth growing each year, it's obvious the craft beer scene here is "hopping." A recent newcomer is Second Wind Brewing Co., and they have wasted no time immersing themselves within the community. Owners Kenny Semcken, Hans Terbush, and J.R. Shepard are avid supporters of the arts and cultural environment within the town, which includes everything from sponsoring Shakespeare in the Park to working with Plymouth Rocks Events on their upcoming exciting town ventures.

Second Wind has already released close to 20 different beers, and with eight tap lines available in their downtown taproom, there is always something on draft to please the most discerning beer palate. The Juggernot extra pale ale imparts flavors of apple, pear, citrus, tropical fruit, tobacco, pepper, and other spice. The Coconut Blackout imperial milk stout is decadent, made with locally sourced 72% dark chocolate, coconut flakes, and whole vanilla beans. And then there's Howland at the Moon witbier, a wheat beer with coriander and zest from fresh citrus of the season.

If you want to take your love of beer one step futher, try cooking with it! The Howland at the Spoon velvety cheese soup (developed by Second Wind's Russ Randall) is perfectly enhanced by Second Wind's Howland wheat beer. This delightful recipe isn't served at the taproom, but it's the perfect crowd-pleasing soup to make for your own get-togethers.

Currently, Second Wind has their beers regularly available at 19+ Plymouth restaurants. But if you want it straight from the source, visit their taproom and outdoor beer garden, located in the heart of historic Plymouth. The unassuming building, tucked back from the street, has been remodeled inside as a slick and sleek space to enjoy some quality flavors. Here, you never know what you might see—from a beer tap that filters through star fruit and kiwis, to buckets of dragon fruit being readied for a new IPA, there's always something fun and interesting going on.

It's been said that the Pilgrims decided to come ashore because they ran out of beer. Well then, Second Wind Brewing Co. is certainly doing its part to fulfill the dreams of our forefathers. Carry on!

Second Wind Brewing Co.

7 Howland Street, Plymouth, MA 02360

Hours: Thur, 5:00–9:00pm;
Fri & Sat, 2:00–9:00pm; Sun, 2:00–7:00pm

secondwindbrewing.com

508-591-5915

HOWLAND AT THE SPOON
(BEER, BRATWURST & CHEDDAR SOUP)

INGREDIENTS

1 red bell pepper

32 oz Crowler of Second Wind's "Howland at the Moon" Witbier

5 bratwurst

2 T olive oil

1 Vidalia onion, finely chopped

1 carrot, finely chopped

1 stalk celery, finely chopped

2 cloves of garlic, finely chopped

¼ C flour

¼ C butter

2 C chicken stock

3 strips of bacon

¼ tsp cayenne pepper

½ tsp ground mustard

2 tsp Worcestershire sauce

2 tsp hot pepper sauce

1 tsp fish sauce

2 medium red russet potatoes, diced into ½-inch cubes

12 oz block of Vermont aged cheddar cheese, grated

1 C heavy cream

1 T chives, finely chopped

DIRECTIONS

1. Preheat the oven to 450°. Place the whole red pepper on a sheet pan and bake for 30 minutes, or until skin begins to char. Remove from oven and when cool enough to handle, de-seed it, chop, and set aside.

2. In a medium stock pot, bring 16 oz of Second Wind "Howland at the Moon" Witbier to a boil, and then reduce heat to medium. Cook bratwurst in the beer for 12 minutes. When done, remove bratwurst from beer, reserving beer for later use.

3. In a large stock pot, heat olive oil on medium. Add onion, carrot, and celery and saute for 4 minutes. Add garlic and saute for 1 minute more.

4. Mix butter and flour together in a small bowl, then whisk into the onion mixture until a thick paste forms. Add chicken stock and whisk until thoroughly combined. Bring to a boil, then reduce to a simmer.

5. Heat a cast iron skillet on medium and cook bacon until crispy. Remove bacon, but keep the pan and grease hot. Roughly chop the bacon and put in your large stock pot.

6. Sear bratwurst in the skillet with the bacon fat, turning every minute until all sides have a nice dark sear. Slice into thin medallions and add to the stock pot.

7. Add the reserved bratwurst beer to your large stock pot. Next, add about ¼ C of the reserved chopped red pepper, as well as the cayenne, mustard powder, Worcestershire, hot pepper sauce, and fish sauce.

8. In another pot, boil potatoes until just undercooked, then strain and add to your large stock pot. Also add 10 oz of the cheese and the heavy cream. Let soup simmer for another 10 minutes.

9. Serve soup and garnish with remaining grated cheddar and chopped chives. Pour the remaining unused beer into a pint glass and drink it!

The Speedwell Tavern

The Speedwell Tavern is all about creating the best comfort food you've ever eaten. Flame-grilled burgers, warm, home-fried potato chips, marinated steak tips, served in a comfortable, casual dining room. Wash it down with one of the most interesting beer selections in town, 24 beers on draft, a curated selection that rotates daily. The tavern is also known for some of the best live music in Plymouth and their fun, lively bar. The house specialty is the chicken wings—23 varieties of sauces and rubs—which have attained legendary status, delicious, unforgettable. You'll come back for them again and again.

The Buffalo Chicken Eggroll recipe was born at their sister restaurant in New Bedford about nine years ago when an over enthusiastic bartender and a hungry bar owner liked to pretend they knew what they were doing in the kitchen. Mysteriously, this dish is now found in pubs everywhere. They don't say at the Speedwell they invented it, but they don't say they didn't! Like the famous schooner this tavern was named for, the Speedwell Tavern is a true original.

The Speedwell Tavern

47 Main Street, Plymouth, MA 02360

Hours: Daily, 11:30AM–1:00AM

speedwellplymouth.com

508-927-4724

INGREDIENTS

2 dozen eggroll wrappers

1 egg and 4 T water (for egg wash)

1 C cornstarch

½ gal vegetable oil for frying

BUFFALO SAUCE:

1 stick butter, melted

1 T garlic powder

1 tsp Lawry's® Seasoned Salt

¼ tsp celery seed

2 C Frank's RedHot® sauce

¼ C white wine vinegar

FILLING:

2 lb boneless, skinless chicken breast, trimmed and cleaned

1 T garlic powder

1 T onion powder

1 tsp Lawry's® Seasoned Salt

4 stalks celery, small diced

1 C carrots, shredded

1 C red onion, small diced

2 C Monterey Jack cheese, shredded

1 C Gorgonzola or bleu cheese, crumbled

1–2 C Buffalo sauce, to taste

salt and pepper, to taste

Buffalo Chicken Eggrolls

DIRECTIONS

1. First, make the Buffalo sauce. Melt the butter in a saucepan. Whisk in dry ingredients. Add Franks RedHot® sauce and vinegar. Whisk until well combined. Set aside to cool in the refrigerator. Note: You will have extra sauce.

2. Preheat oven to 375°. Combine the garlic powder, onion powder, and seasoned salt. Rub over the chicken to season it well. Bake for 15 minutes (or completely cooked inside). Let cool, then cut into small dice and put in refrigerator to get cold.

3. After chicken and Buffalo sauce have had a chance to get cold, again preheat the oven to 375°.

4. Next make the filling. Combine the vegetables, cold diced chicken, cheeses, and cold Buffalo sauce in a large container. Mix well.

5. Next assemble the eggrolls. Put about ¼ cup of filling in the middle of the eggroll wrapper in a log shape, but not touching edges (fig 1) and then fold bottom corner over filling (fig 2).

6. Use your egg wash to moisten the top corner and about 2 inches in each direction of the top of the eggroll wrapper. Fold sides in as shown (fig 3). Carefully roll toward the top flap, keeping it tight without ripping (fig 4), until you've rolled over the top flap and made sure it is securely sealed (fig 5).

Note: Coat them in cornstarch if you're not frying them immediately to prevent them from sticking together, and this provides some additional crunch during frying.

7. Heat oil in a deep fryer or wok to 350°. Be sure to not fill too high to prevent boil over.

8. When oil is up to temp, drop one or two eggrolls in at a time. Gently move them around with a slotted spoon to prevent sticking. Do not overcrowd.

9. Fry for 6–8 minutes, then let drain on paper towels.

10. Cut eggrolls in half diagonally. Filling should be melty and hot! Serve with a side of your favorite bleu cheese or ranch dressing for dipping and some celery sticks to cool you off!

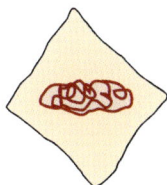

fig 1

fig 2

fig 3

fig 4

fig 5

Stracco's Subs & More

Walking into Stracco's Subs & More is like walking into your neighbor's home where Italian cooking is all about loving people. They love what they do, and they do a fabulous job. This family-owned restaurant is one of the friendliest in Plymouth. Rico and his wife Antonietta work side by side with their children Marc, Olivia, and Rico. A trip into Stracco's is a sensory pleasure. The scent of good red sauce reminds you that everything is made from scratch here, from family recipes. The quality shows in every dish. The subs here are fresh and mouth-watering, from a traditional Sicilian—meatballs and Italian sausage with peppers, onions, marinara sauce, and mozzarella cheese; to the unexpected Baby Ree—grilled orange chicken with mandarin sauce and chow mein noodles.

Both takeout and delivery are available. And it's easy to stop off here and pick up a healthy dinner for your family, with generous portions and nicely priced. Stracco's is small, but enjoying a Pilgrim sub made from their own oven-roasted turkey, at an outside table on a summer afternoon, is a real treat. Or take your feast over to the harbor for waterfront dining with food that rivals any restaurant you might find in Boston's North End. Regulars here talk about not having to deal with Boston traffic and rave about how "the best meatballs in New England are now right here in Plymouth." Whatever you order, you'll keep coming back until you've tried everything. And no matter how full you are, you'll want dessert. Rico's long career at the well-known Montilio's Baking Co. explains the tantalizing cannolis. His Lobster Tail with a Bavarian cream, ricotta, and whipped cream filling is spectacular.

Dinners here are yummy. Rico's Arancini (stuffed rice balls) are the best of all worlds. A golden brown and lightly crispy outer rice coating covers a delicious meatball filling. Perfection! And don't miss the eggplant Parmigiana and ravioli just like your Italian grandmother used to make—if you had an Italian grandmother. And if you didn't, don't despair because once you step inside the door of Stracco's, you'll know you've discovered family, and some of the best Italian food you've ever tasted. Mangia!

Stracco's Subs & More

85 Sandwich Street, Plymouth, MA 02360

Hours: Mon–Wed, 10:00AM–6:00PM

Thur & Fri, 10:00AM–7:00PM

Sat, 10:00AM–5:00PM

straccossubs.com

774-343-5968

ARANCINI (STUFFED RICE BALLS)

DIRECTIONS

1. Cook the rice according to packaging directions, until completely tender.

2. While rice is cooking, prepare the filling. First, sauté the ground beef in the olive oil. After it has browned, drain off the excess grease and set aside.

3. In a large bowl, combine the peas, mozzarella, Romano, salt and pepper, and 1 C marinara sauce. Add the cooked ground beef and mix well to combine.

4. In another bowl, whisk the eggs.

5. In another bowl, place your seasoned bread crumbs.

6. After the rice has cooled enough to handle, shape the rice into balls, about the size of an orange. The rice should be sticky and hold together. Form all the rice into balls.

7. Take each ball and funnel a hole into the center with your thumb. Then take a few tablespoons of filling and place into the hole. Be careful not to overfill. Seal the hole over carefully with rice and make sure the rice is securely in place around the filling.

8. Coat each rice ball lightly with the eggs, and then carefully dredge in the bread crumbs.

9. Heat your oil up to temp for deep frying. Use a large enough frying receptacle so as not to overcrowd. You want the balls to be able to float. A wok or deep fryer works best. Fry the rice balls, carefully turning occasionally until golden brown.

10. Serve covered with marinara sauce and cheese. Enjoy!

INGREDIENTS

1 (32 oz) bag of medium-grain rice

3 eggs

1 lb seasoned bread crumbs

oil for deep frying

2 C marinara sauce

½ C Romano cheese

FILLING:

1 lb ground beef

2 T olive oil

half a (1 lb) bag of frozen peas

¾ C mozzarella cheese

½ C Romano cheese

salt and pepper, to taste

1 C marinara sauce

Surfside Smokehouse

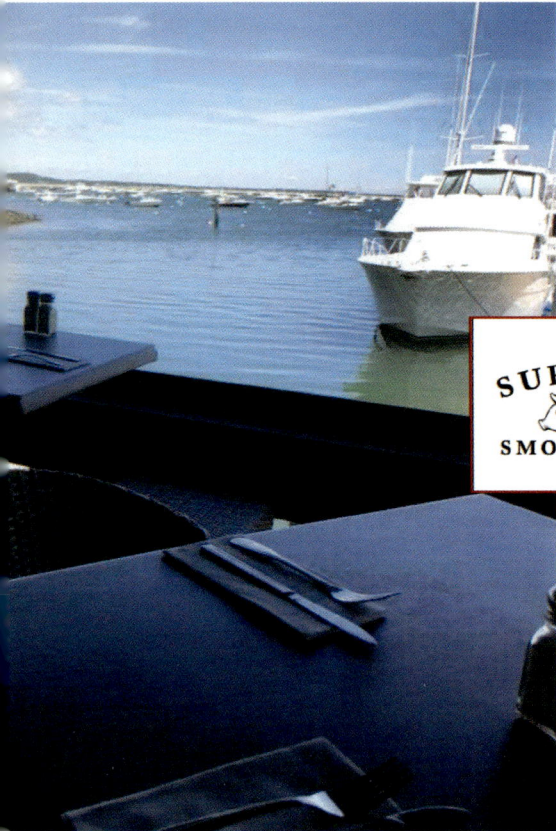

The first time you dine at the Surfside Smokehouse, all you can say is *wow*! This restaurant at Brewer's Plymouth Marina is placed perfectly on Plymouth Harbor. Dining al fresco on a summer day, your view stretches out overlooking both the Rock and the *Mayflower II*, with Cole's Hill stretching up to the sky on one side, and the dazzling blue Atlantic on the other. They have one of the best views in Plymouth, but the Surfside Smokehouse is much more than just a pretty place. It's about fabulous food and a wonderful waitstaff.

Check out the menu and you'll discover a winning combination of fresh seafood and authentic southern barbeque. From the Carolina pulled pork to the Memphis pork ribs, you'll find yourself in meat lover's paradise. Pork is smoked in-house overnight for 12 to 14 hours, served with all the fixings—grilled street corn, their signature mac and cheese, and cornbread. Then you have a seafood lover's nirvana—blackened salmon tacos with guacamole, cilantro sour cream, and salsa verde. The fried shrimp platter is traditional and tasty. Or mix it up with their marvelous Smokehouse jambalaya.

The Surfside Smokehouse has a popular outdoor bar on the deck—the perfect place to sip a bloody Mary as you watch the big yachts pull up, or linger over their luscious bread pudding with bourbon-glazed ice cream. This is also a great place to bring the family. Kids have a fun time here enjoying the kids sweet BBQ pulled pork sliders.

Owners Fred Bisaillon and Denise Corson have built on their expertise running their Nantucket restaurants, B-ACK Yard BBQ and the legendary The Charlie Noble, to create the Surfside Smokehouse. Executive Chef Andrew Nelson makes everything in-house and fresh seafood comes in daily. There is music on the weekends and a creative Sunday brunch menu. Denise Corson generously shared her recipe for Kielbasa & Pineapple Spiced "Candy" with us, an ideal blend of sweet and salty. Nibble on this perfect appetizer while you watch the sun set. Whether you're a local or a tourist, every meal feels like a vacation.

Surfside Smokehouse

14 Union Street, Plymouth, MA 02360

Hours:
Sun–Thu, 11:30AM–9:00PM (bar 10:00PM)
Fri & Sat, 11:30AM–9:30PM (bar 10:30PM)

surfsidesmokehouse.com

508-927-4111

KIELBASA & PINEAPPLE SPICED "CANDY"

DIRECTIONS

1. First, clean the pineapple. Stand it on its end and slice off the outer peel in strips from top to bottom. Then cut thick slices off until you reach the core. Discard the core and peel. Cut the slices into 1-inch cubes.

2. Slice the kielbasa into bite-sized rounds.

3. In a bowl, mix the pineapple juice, brown sugar, and sambal.

4. Heat a large sauté pan over medium-high heat, then sear the kielbasa and pineapple pieces until the pineapple starts to caramelize and turn golden.

5. Add the sauce mixture and simmer until reduced by half.

SERVING VARIATIONS: This makes enough for a party-sized appetizer. If you are cooking for less, you could easily halve this recipe and serve with white or yellow (Spanish) rice for a wonderful dinner for four.

FOODIE FACT

Pineapples are actually very easy to grow yourself in pots, even indoors. They need little care or water, as they do not have a large root system. They do, however, take a very long time to produce a fruit—about 2 years! If you want to try yourself, cut off the top of a store-bought pineapple, remove any flesh and small leaves at the bottom, and simply plant in a large pot of soil mixed with compost. Mulch thickly around the plant. Water occasionally on the leafy area, and make sure the soil does not get soggy. Plant in a sunny area.

INGREDIENTS

1 ripe pineapple

6 C pineapple juice

4 C brown sugar

2 T sambal (hot chili paste)

4 (14-oz) links smoked kielbasa

TAR BAR

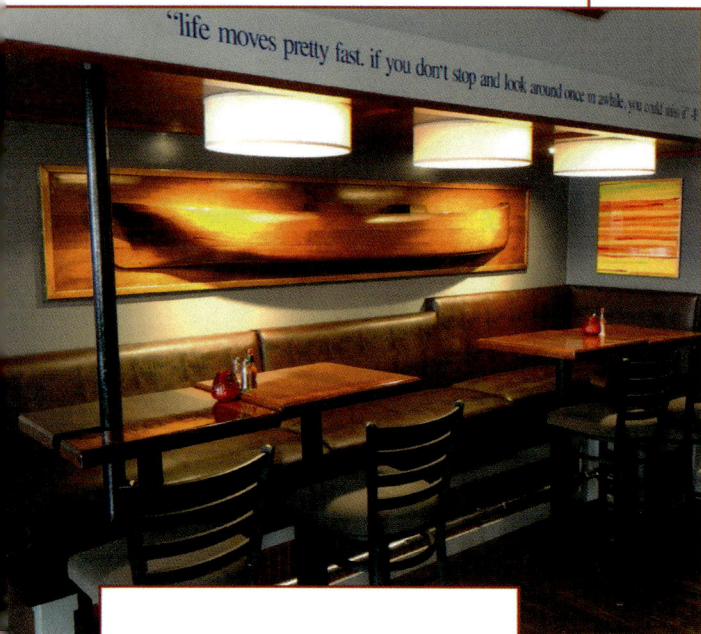

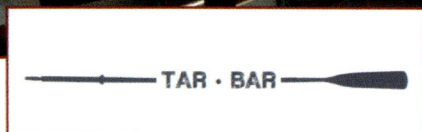

TAR BAR on Court Street is one of Plymouth's newest casual-fare pubs. Comfortable, warm, with great service and bartenders who are pros, this is an inviting place to settle down for the evening and enjoy some delicious food.

First off, the name—TAR BAR, as you might imagine, could mean many things. *Tar* actually means *a sailor.* Managing partner Taylor Currier told us that he wanted to incorporate Plymouth's seafaring history into his restaurant. The TAR BAR name honors all that celebrates the high seas. His concept of a "dive in denial" just means a simple bar that strives to be more. And this establishment is definitely more, as seen in the classy nautical décor, which includes a gorgeous teak ceiling, to the artwork details, such as the sailboat painting behind the bar.

The menu is also elevated. Interesting appetizers such as Cranberry Hummus, yummy and easy-to make, add an eclectic element. This house-made hummus uses goat cheese and dried cranberries, and is served with fried pita bread, carrots, and celery.

Entrees include the TAR BAR burger that comes with a fried egg, bacon, cheddar, tomato, lettuce, and maple aioli. The lobster grilled cheese with bacon reinvents a classic. Side choices are French fries, sweet potato fries, or coleslaw. And Buffalo chicken or lobster can be added to their comfort food mac 'n cheese. Stuffed pretzels are also exceptional here. Try the Reuben pretzel—Guinness-braised corned beef, cider-simmered sauerkraut, and Swiss cheese, served with Russian dressing—different and satisfying. A recent day found a homemade meatball special, so good we hope it finds a home on the regular menu. Don't leave without trying the fried Oreo dessert—deep-fried Oreos, chocolate ice cream, whipped cream, chocolate sauce, and powdered sugar—a sweet-tooth delight!

There is a nice selection of specialty cocktails, wine, and beer, including local brews. Events include live music and open-mic nights. Become a regular at TAR BAR and enjoy the fun atmosphere, casual and cozy vibe, and out-of-the-ordinary yummy food.

TAR BAR

47 Court Street, Plymouth, MA 02360

Hours: Mon–Wed, 4:00PM–1:00AM
Thur–Sun:,11:30AM–1:00AM

tarbarplymouth.com

774-343-5623

CRANBERRY HUMMUS

DIRECTIONS

1. Combine the chickpeas, olive oil, tahini paste, lemon juice, cranberry sauce, minced garlic, cumin, onion powder, salt, and pepper in a food processor or blender.
2. Blend hummus a few minutes, until completely smooth.
3. In a bowl, combine the goat cheese, dried cranberries, and parsley.
4. Place your hummus in a serving bowl, and top with a bit of the cheese mixture.

Serve with lightly fried pita bread, carrots, and celery.

INGREDIENTS

4 C canned chickpeas, rinsed and drained

¼ C olive oil

1 C tahini paste

1 C lemon juice

21 oz jellied cranberry sauce

1 T minced garlic

2 T cumin

1 T onion powder

salt and pepper, to taste

¾ C crumbled goat cheese

¾ C dried cranberries

2 T fresh parsley, chopped

Tavern on the Wharf

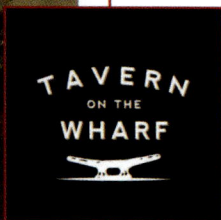

The beautiful and traditional Tavern on the Wharf has become a popular go-to destination for locals and tourists alike. Great, affordable food, water views from almost every seat in the house, family-friendly but also perfect for an event or date night. There is so much to love about this award-winning restaurant. While enjoying Chef Victor Viera's special Wharf Clam Chowder you can watch local fishermen unloading their daily catch, and the interesting activity in historic Plymouth Harbor. You'll want to return again and again for some of the freshest seafood on the coast and this wonderful panoramic view.

The buzz around town is that the best fried calamari in Plymouth is found here. The pan-seared salmon is topped with pineapple mango salsa and served with jasmine rice and sautéed spinach, a perfect seaside dinner. And don't miss the time-honored baked New England cod. The delicious herb-encrusted cod is served alongside a vegetable risotto and a mouth-watering lemon butter sauce. It's hard to step away from their seafood, but if you find yourself here on a cool, foggy night, order the chicken pot pie or bacon-wrapped meatloaf served with red bliss mashed potatoes—divine comfort foods.

The Tavern on the Wharf has become a great place to host a function. A wedding reception or an event of any kind becomes a real celebration with the expertise of the dedicated Tavern staff. Different function areas are available with seating for up to 300. A separate dining room with access to a 50-seat outdoor patio is a wonderful choice for private parties.

There is a fun bar with a full selection of drafts and wine, and all kinds of weekly events—happy hour specials, taco Tuesdays, and live music on Friday and Saturday. Kids love it here and eat free on Mondays with your purchase of an adult entrée. Craft cocktails feature fresh fruits and infusions. From Sunday brunch buffet to Friday and Saturday king cut prime rib nights, the wide selection of outstanding food makes any visit to the Tavern on the Wharf an unforgettable dining experience.

Tavern on the Wharf

6 Town Wharf, Plymouth, MA 02360

Hours: Mon–Wed, 11:00AM–10:00PM

Thur, 11:00AM–11:00PM

Fri–Sat, 11:00AM–12:00AM

Sun, 10:00AM–10:00PM

tavernonthewharf.com

508-927-4961

Wharf Clam Chowder

DIRECTIONS

1. To a large stock pot, add the 4 oz butter, onions, celery, and garlic and cook for a few minutes.

2. To the pot, add the clams and sauté until fully cooked, about 5 minutes.

3. To the pot, add the wine, clam bouillon, thyme, parsley, and pepper. Cook for about 7 minutes.

4. Next, add water and potatoes to the pot. Bring back to a boil and cook until potatoes are fork tender, about 6–8 minutes. Then turn to low heat.

5. In a large saucepan, melt the 2 C butter and add the flour to make a roux. Whisk until fully mixed and cook for about 3 minutes, whisking occasionally.

6. Add some chowder to the roux to thin it out a bit, then pour this entire mixture into the chowder pot. Mix well, stirring occasionally for about 5 minutes.

7. Add the cream to the pot and stir well. Bring to a slight simmer, then turn off heat. It is ready to serve.

NOTE: This makes a large pot of chowder, enough for about 24 servings, perfect for a party or gathering!

FOODIE FACT

Clams can live for about 35 years, if they escape your dinner plate. The giant clam, the world's largest living bivalve mollusk, can actually live for more than 150 years. Since clams don't have a brain, eyes, ears, or noses, how do you suppose they occupy themselves all those years? It's been surmised that a clam has only two goals in life: to eat and to reproduce, hence the phrase "happy as a clam."

INGREDIENTS

4 oz unsalted butter	2 T thyme
1 large onion, diced	4 T parsley
2 stalks celery, diced	1 T black pepper
¼ C garlic, chopped	7 C water
2½ lb chopped clams	6 C potatoes, peeled and cubed
½ C white wine	2 C butter (for roux)
4 T Better Than Bouillon® clam base	2 C flour (for roux)
	7 C light cream

T-Bones Road House

When you walk into T-Bones Road House, you feel like you've just moseyed into Texas. Take a look around at the bar and you'll expect a cowboy to be chugging down a whiskey, straight up. The Wild West vibe here is fun and comfortable, and the food is delicious. It's a great place to sink into one of their extra-cozy booths and spend a few hours enjoying everything their great menu has to offer.

Start with the skillet cornbread, served in a small cast-iron pan with plenty of cinnamon honey butter. Perfect with their Road House Chili, some of the best chili you've had anywhere. Saddle up with one of their sandwiches served on a grilled roll, and ask for their special sweet potato fries or onion rings. The Southwest chicken sandwich is topped with pepper Jack cheese and guacamole. Or maybe choose the Texas steak dip—shaved prime rib, American cheese, and sautéed onions in a grilled flour tortilla, served with au jus. The Road House shows off its style with their rodeo rib dinner—a slow-smoked, St. Louis-style half rack of ribs, slathered in house BBQ sauce, smoked daily, and served with two sides. Try the sweet slaw and Mexican rice. Their fresh-off-the-grill entrees are the stuff of every cowboy's dream—bourbon steak tips are flame-grilled Angus steak generously covered with their signature sweet bourbon glaze. And don't miss the San Antonio—a center-cut 8-oz filet mignon, seasoned and flame-grilled to perfection.

The large rectangle bar will remind you of a scene from the movie *High Noon* and it's a lively place on a Sunday afternoon. The hanging basket seats by the window facing Main Street are an entertaining place to take in the local scenery. T-Bones has a loyal following for their affordable breakfasts, served seven days a week, with lots of specials. There's live music and events throughout the week—taco Tuesdays, with an all-you-can-eat taco and nacho bar from 5:00 to 10:00PM. Don't miss Thursday evenings, when the purchase of a margarita gets you a free fajita. You'll enjoy your visit to T-Bones Road House, a little bit of Dodge City in Plymouth center.

T-Bones Road House

22 Main Street, Plymouth, MA 02360

Hours: Daily, 8:00AM–1:00AM

tbonesroadhouse.com

508-747-2667

ROAD HOUSE CHILI

DIRECTIONS

1. In a large pot, brown the beef, then drain off the excess fat.
2. Combine all other ingredients with the beef, except the beans. Let simmer over low heat for one hour or more, until desired consistency is reached. It should get thicker as it cooks. Stir occasionally so it doesn't stick to the bottom of the pot.
3. Rinse the canned beans and stir into the chili. Simmer another 20 minutes.

Serve with your favorite chili garnishes, such as cheddar cheese, sour cream, and tortilla chips. Enjoy!

Serves 8.

FOODIE FACT

According to the International Chili Society, the first chili cook-off took place in 1967 in Terlinga, Texas, a border town about 400 miles west of chili's alleged birthplace, San Antonio. It ended in a tie between a native Texan and, surprisingly, a New Yorker. Chili cook-offs are popular nationwide today.

INGREDIENTS

2 lb ground beef

½ C onions, diced

½ C red and green peppers, diced

2 tsp garlic, minced

1 fresh jalapeño, minced

2 T ground cumin

2 T chili powder

2 T Ancho chili powder

1 tsp cayenne

1 tsp black pepper

½ tsp kosher salt

1 T brown sugar

1½ C beef broth

1 tsp sriracha sauce

1 tsp chipotle puree

1½ lb diced tomatoes in sauce

1½ lb canned red kidney beans

Top Crust Pizza

Top Crust Pizzeria & Deli is on every list of Plymouth's best pizza and their reputation is well-deserved. We all have an opinion on what makes a great pizza, there are so many choices and we love to discuss the topic. The New York–style pizza made by Top Crust is a real crowd-pleaser. The crust is thin and just a little crisp along the edge, the wide slices sturdy, yet soft enough to be easily folded, the perfect pizza to be eaten with your hands and with gusto. One bite and you know you'll be happily reaching for another slice.

This pizzeria makes its own dough and sauce, and you can tell the difference. Nothing is frozen, no short-cut measures here. You may choose a traditional tomato sauce to adorn your pizza and it will be absolutely delicious. They also make a yummy gluten-free pizza, not easy to find.

Select a basic Margherita (cheese pizza) and add the toppings you prefer—fresh veggies, roasted veggies, meats, seafood, and special cheeses. Or you may choose one of the Top Crust specialties. They include the Plymouth Rock—pepperoni, extra mozzarella, and fresh garlic; or perhaps the Court Street—a red sauce pizza with chorizo, jalapeño peppers, and fresh garlic; and don't miss the Light House—breaded eggplant, sun-dried tomato, with red sauce. Wrap sandwiches, wine, and beer are also available.

The Garden Pesto Pizza is a creative blend of diced tomato, asiago cheese, fresh garlic, and artichoke hearts with a pesto base. Owner Al Carvelli was very kind to give us their recipe but don't wait to make it yourself, come into the pizzeria tonight and watch Chef Moises Rodriguez ("Jerry") build the pizza by hand and slide it into the oven. Kids will have fun here at this family-friendly restaurant. A former U.S. Navy pilot, Al Carvelli displays his proud collection of model airplanes in glass cases along the wall. Kids will love admiring the famous "Old Crow B6" and the "Fighting 84" among many others.

Don't leave without dessert—cannolis filled by hand with chocolate-chip ricotta cream. The perfect finish to a perfect pizza at Top Crust.

Top Crust Pizzeria & Deli

15 Court Street, Plymouth, MA 02360

Hours: Sun–Thur, 11:30AM–8:00PM
Fri & Sat, 11:30AM–10:00PM

topcrustpizza.com

508-747-6000

New York–Style Garden Pesto Pizza

DIRECTIONS

1. Preheat the oven to 450°. If you are using a pizza stone, put it in the oven now and make sure it has enough time to achieve the needed temperature.

2. Flatten the dough out a bit to disk shape, then spread the flour over both sides of the dough and start stretching it by hand, to form your pizza. Use more flour if needed to keep it from getting too sticky.

3. Use a rolling pin to roll out the crust to your final round shape(s).

4. Place pizza dough onto your pizza pan. If you are using a pizza stone, you will build your pizza on your pizza paddle instead, so that you can slide it onto your stone after it's built.

5. Mix the garlic, olive oil, and pesto and spread over the crust to within about an inch of the edge.

6. Spread the tomatoes over the pesto. Next, spread on the mozzarella. Next, spread on the artichoke hearts.

7. Sprinkle the entire pizza with the dried basil and dried garlic.

8. Spread the asiago cheese over the other toppings. Brush a little olive oil over that 1-inch bare edge of your crust.

9. Bake for approximately 6–8 minutes, or until your desired crispiness. The longer you leave it in, the crispier the crust will become.

Makes one 18-inch pizza, or two 9-inch pizzas.

FOODIE FACT

What is New York–style pizza? If you've been lucky enough to have had the New York pizza experience, you'll know that New York–style pizza is generally a thin, flexible crust, light on sauce and toppings, cut into large slices.

INGREDIENTS

20 oz premade pizza dough, thawed

1 C flour

2 T fresh garlic, minced

1 T olive oil

3 T basil pesto

1 C tomatoes, diced

10 oz shredded mozzarella cheese

1 C quartered artichoke hearts

1 tsp dried basil flakes

1 tsp dried minced garlic

2 oz shredded asiago cheese

Water Street Café

Ask anyone in Plymouth where you can get a great breakfast, and Water Street Café will come up again and again. In 2018, owners Lisa and P.J. O'Hanley celebrated their 20th year in business. Their expertise in the food industry shows in every dish they serve. From Chef P.J.'s homemade corned beef hash, to his perfect pancakes—take your pick from blueberry, strawberry, chocolate chip, or banana—everything is made from scratch and cooked to order. P.J. imports gallons of pure maple syrup from Vermont to complement his Belgian waffles and banana bread French toast.

Water Street Café has been a family-run business from the start. All three of the kids have worked here through the years. Lisa's mother, Marcey Romboldi, was the baker until she passed away in 2010, and they still make her scrumptious Orange-Cranberry Scones, the perfect accompaniment to their mushroom, onion, and cheddar omelet.

This cozy, sunlit restaurant has plenty of parking, and some say the friendliest waitstaff around. Even though they're known for their amazing breakfasts, don't forget to plan a lunch date here. Daily specials entice as do house favorites, such as the Thanksgiving wrap—sliced turkey, stuffing, and cranberry sauce in a tortilla wrap. Don't miss the Donovan—grilled ham and Swiss cheese topped with fresh baby spinach and garlic mayo on focaccia bread.

Grab a window seat and you can enjoy the beautiful view of Brewster Gardens, while sipping your morning coffee. The two bright and sunny dining rooms will be filled with locals, business owners, travelers, and even the famous have been known to stop in when they're in town. Celebrity watchers have caught sight of Emmy Award-winning actor and star of *Taxi*, Judd Hirsch; and actor Eric Stoltz, whose numerous credits include *Pulp Fiction*, *Chicago Hope*, and *Mad About You*. Aside from occasional celebrities, politicians have also been known to lunch here while on the campaign trail. Everyone is welcome and the menu has something delicious for all tastes.

Water Street Café

25 Water Street, Plymouth, MA 02360

Hours: Breakfast and lunch daily, 5:30AM–3:00PM

waterstreetcafeplymouth.com

508-746-2050

ORANGE-CRANBERRY SCONES

DIRECTIONS

1. Preheat oven to 350°.
2. In a large bowl, combine the flour, sugar, baking powder, baking soda, and salt. Add the grated orange rind to the bowl as well.
3. Cut the butter into tablespoon-sized chunks, then add them to the bowl of dry ingredients. Cut in by hand, using a fork or pastry blender, until the mixture forms into pea-sized balls.
4. Pour buttermilk into the bowl and mix with a spoon, by hand.
5. Add the dried cranberries to the bowl and mix until just incorporated.
6. Form the dough into a ball, and place onto a lightly floured counter top. Cut into 2 even pieces.
7. Form the 2 pieces into two disks, about ½-inch thick. Then cut each disk, pizza-style, into 8 wedges each.
8. Butter a sheet pan (do not use cooking spray). Place all 16 wedges on the pan and brush them lightly with the egg wash.
9. Bake at 350° for 8 minutes, turn pan and then bake for another 8 minutes, until just golden.

FOODIE FACT

"Cutting in" means incorporating the butter into the flour so that little pea-sized lumps of butter remain within the flour mixture. When the dough is baked, these little lumps create pockets in the final product, which is what gives it that flaky consistency.

INGREDIENTS

6 C all-purpose flour

¾ C granulated sugar

5 tsp baking powder

1 tsp baking soda

1 tsp salt

1 orange rind, grated

1½ C cold butter

2 C buttermilk

2 C dried cranberries

egg wash (1 or 2 beaten eggs)

Waterfront Bar & Grill

Combine an amazing location with ocean views, excellent food and drink, upstairs and downstairs decks and bars, nightly entertainment, and a superb function facility and you wonder how anyone can do so many things right. At the Waterfront Bar & Grill, they manage to juggle all these amenities to create widespread excellence.

In warm weather, the upstairs deck is a great place for lunch, brunch, or dinner—spacious and elegant, yet casual and relaxed, with amazing views. People look up from the street and immediately want to eat outside on the top deck. But there's an outside deck and bar downstairs too, so it's hard to choose. Inside there's a quiet, downstairs dining room and bar, great for that special date or business lunch, and the perfect function space for up to 60 guests. Upstairs there's a large dining room and huge bar that provide a great view in all weather, plus entertainment, superb dining, and drinks.

The menu is nicely balanced with popular favorites, great salads, soups, and appetizers—such as their signature Stuffed Quahog, shared here—as well as lunch, brunch, and wonderful dinner entrees. There's a very American feel to the menu with a great seafood section that includes char-grilled swordfish with blueberry and strawberry salsa, hand-battered fish and chips, and grilled salmon with lemon and dill. The emphasis is on fresh, simple, high-quality ingredients.

There's a delicious selection of steakhouse cuts, such as steak tips, New York sirloin, surf and turf, and braised, slow-roasted short ribs that are mouth-watering and tender. There is even a grilled pork chop topped with a bourbon, maple, and cherry pepper demi-glace. Visit a few times and you'll notice that the whipped potatoes and asparagus are always perfectly done.

Lunch and Sunday brunch are amazing and, of course, there are great desserts. Their crème brûlée is a favorite. There are special menus for functions that make planning a breeze. Try the Waterfront Bar & Grill when you want to see Plymouth Harbor from a delicious vantage point.

Waterfront Bar & Grill

170 Water Street (at Village Landing), Plymouth, MA 02360

Hours: Daily, 11:30AM–1:00AM

plymouthwaterfront.com

508-591-8393

STUFFED QUAHOGS

DIRECTIONS

1. Preheat the oven to 400°.

2. In a medium pot, bring 4 cups water to a boil over high heat. Place the quahogs in the pot and let them steam until they open, about 5–6 minutes. Remove the quahogs and strain the water from the pot (which is now quahog broth) and save it for later use.

3. Next, remove the clam meat from the shells. When cool, chop into chunky ¼-inch pieces, or use a food processor. Set aside the shells for later use.

4. In a large skillet over medium-high heat, add the butter, linguiça (or chorizo), onions, bell pepper, black pepper, and red pepper flakes and cook until the vegetables become translucent. Add the chopped quahog meat, and cook for 3–4 minutes longer.

5. In a large mixing bowl, add the reserved quahog broth to the croutons. Add the parsley and fold together. When the croutons have absorbed the broth, add the hot ingredients to the bowl. Incorporate all of the ingredients, and add enough plain bread crumbs until the mixture is stiff.

6. Divide the mixture into 10 even balls, about 5 ounces each, or 3 inches in diameter, and place firmly into the set aside shells. Place the shells on a sheet pan and into the oven until the outside of the quahog is golden brown.

Serves 10.

INGREDIENTS

10 large live quahogs

1 lb butter

1 lb ground linguiça or chorizo

1 pureed onion

1 pureed red bell pepper

1 tsp black pepper

1 tsp crushed red pepper flakes

12 oz plain croutons

2 T fresh parsley

3 to 5 oz plain bread crumbs

Will & Co. Café

Will & Co. Café might be the most fun eatery in Plymouth. The happy energy here is contagious. This is a place where the whole family works together and has a great time. Chef Tom Bissett has been making some of the Café's dishes for over 30 years. Cooking alongside his son Jason Bissett, the two of them together have over 55 years of experience running kitchens.

Every family member has a breakfast dish named for them. Grandpa's Red Flannel Hash is a good example. Grandpa Tom's secret corned beef hash recipe is served with two poached eggs, cornbread, home fries, and baked beans—a time-honored and terrific recipe.

You might catch mom Karen waitressing and cutting a large piece of Jason's luscious, Oreo Brownie Lava Cake for a diner. You'll definitely want to try Sharon's Favorite, a slice of their amazing raspberry French toast and a slice of their white bread French toast, served with homemade warm raspberry Chambord syrup and sausage.

Everything is made to order, nothing is pre-made, and they have vegan and gluten-free choices. Their quiches are becoming legendary. If you love quiche, it's a must-try. The Eggs Florentine is a delightful combination of portobello mushrooms, spinach, and perfectly cooked eggs with a hollandaise sauce that is heavenly.

Comfy booths make this a place where you'll want to linger over an amazing cup of coffee. Jason's wife Brooke has added a contemporary flair. Her love for a great cup of coffee brought organic beans and fair-trade tea and her dream is to bring in a coffee roaster and roast and brew her own coffee. We can hardly wait.

The Will & Co. Café is an exciting mixture of the traditional and the new. Lunches here include meatloaf melts as well as the exotic Mayflower Benedict—wild caught lobster in a garlic butter sauce with grilled steak tips on a croissant, with two poached eggs and hollandaise sauce. Wow! Recently, Scott Simonson, NFL player for the Carolina Panthers, was seen here enjoying this mouth-watering dish. Celebrities, tourists, businessmen, friends . . . It's all one big family at the Will & Co. Café.

Will & Co. Café
6b Court Street, Plymouth, MA 02360
Hours: Mon–Fri, 7:30AM–3:00PM
Sat & Sun, 7:30AM–2:30PM
774-773-9732

Eggs Florentine

DIRECTIONS

1. First, make the hollandaise sauce. Melt the 1 cup butter. It should be hot but not boiling.
2. Place the 6 egg yolks in food processor or blender. Turn on to medium speed, then slowly drizzle in the melted butter. You don't want your yolks to scramble, so add the butter slowly. When incorporated, turn off your processor or blender.
3. Add the lemon juice and hot pepper sauce. Stir lightly and set aside.
4. Place water in a medium saucepan, and bring to a boil.
5. Carefully crack the 4 eggs into the water for poaching. Cook for 2 minutes then remove pan from heat, but leave eggs in the water.
6. Place 1 tsp of butter in separate sauté pan over medium heat. When butter has melted, add the onions, mushrooms, and spinach. Cook for 1–2 minutes covered, until spinach has steamed.
7. Remove from heat and add salt and pepper to taste.
8. Add the garlic and mix.
9. Divide the spinach mixture onto two plates, then top with the cheddar cheese.
10. With a slotted spoon, remove your eggs from the hot water, and gently place on top of the spinach and cheese. Top with the hollandaise sauce and enjoy!

Serves 2.

FOODIE FACT

Did you know that Eggs Florentine is a variation of Eggs Benedict? There are many other variations as well, including Eggs Chesapeake that uses Maryland blue crab cakes, Eggs Trivette that adds Creole mustard and crayfish, Eggs Hemingway that uses salmon, and Eggs Blanchard that substitutes béchamel sauce for the hollandaise. How would you put your special twist on this classic recipe?

INGREDIENTS

4 eggs

1 tsp butter

1 T onion, minced

1 C portobello mushrooms, sliced

5 C spinach

½ tsp garlic, minced

salt and pepper, to taste

½ C shredded cheddar cheese

HOLLANDAISE SAUCE:

1 C butter

6 egg yolks

a quarter of a lemon, squeezed

½ tsp hot pepper sauce

Wood's Seafood

wood's
seafood

If you're a seafood lover traveling to Plymouth, a stop at Wood's Seafood on Town Pier is a must. This local institution serves the freshest seafood available. A fish market *and* casual restaurant, you'll find everyone has their own Wood's story—coming here with your parents on a Friday night for a heaping plate of mouth-watering golden fried clams; many had their first taste of lobster here; or the young woman who dines here every year with her grandfather on his birthday, enjoying crab cakes and fries, a delicious memory she'll keep forever.

Jay Kimball has owned Wood's since 1989 and he's developed a close relationship to the local fishing community. You'll find Jay working hard, buying lobsters right off the boat and proud of the reputation that Wood's has earned. Everything about Wood's is simple and easy. Check out the menu on the wall, order at the counter, wait to hear your number called, and then enjoy your feast while watching the incredible water view right outside the window. In addition, they ship live lobsters, clambakes, and chowders across the United States. Among the many choices available are fresh salmon, scrod, haddock, filet of sole, swordfish, shrimp, and of course, Jay's wonderful Homemade Fishcakes.

Jay shared a bit of the history of these fishcakes with us. Fishcakes have been around forever. Way back, they were made using salted cod from Canada. The cod was soaked in water to remove the salt, then boiled, drained, refrigerated, and then potatoes added. Times have changed. Now, Wood's is one of the few places in eastern Massachusetts to still make their own homemade fishcakes. Jay uses only cod, haddock, or flounder. When a customer comes into the market to purchase fish, sometimes there's a small piece left over. Rather than throw this away, Wood's uses it as the main ingredient for fishcakes or chowder. Reducing waste in fresh seafood says a lot about the conscious way Wood's operates. And these fishcakes are great! Wood's has been voted a *Yankee Magazine* Editor's Choice, New England seafood at its best.

Wood's Seafood

15 Town Pier, Plymouth, MA 02360

Hours: Daily, year-round
Fish Market from 9:00AM–7:00PM
Restaurant from 11:00AM–8:00PM

woodsseafoods.com

508-746-0261

HOMEMADE FISHCAKES

DIRECTIONS

1. Simmer fish in unsalted water for approximately 15 minutes, until fish turns white and flakes. Drain and refrigerate until ready to use.

2. Boil potatoes until completely soft. Drain and break apart by hand with a sturdy wisk. Do not mash. Set aside to cool.

3. When fish and potatoes have cooled, mix them together by hand. Add one beaten egg, which helps to bind them together. Add the white pepper and a dash of salt.

4. Spread the mixture onto a clean surface and level the mixture to 1 inch in thickness. Use a 2½-inch or 3-inch ring to cut out the fishcakes. Once the portion is in your hands, you can mold it and make completely round, so it's not so flat.

5. Cover the entire fishcake with a store bought clam-fry mixture (or make your own with cornmeal mixed with flour).

6. Heat up enough oil for your fishcakes in a wok or deep fryer. When up to temp (375°), gently slide the fishcakes in with a slotted spoon, and fry until golden brown. When done, transfer them to a cooling rack covered with paper towels, to drain off excess oil.

7. You may serve these immediately; or, if you want to prepare these ahead of time, you should cool them on the cooling rack for about 30 minutes. Then, transfer to the refrigerator. To reheat, place fishcakes on a baking sheet and heat at 350° for about 15 minutes.

Serve with your favorite tartar or cocktail sauce, and sides such as coleslaw or corn on the cob. A true New England classic.

INGREDIENTS

2 lb fresh fish (cod, haddock, hake, or similar white fish)

2 lb peeled potatoes, quartered

1 egg, beaten

1 tsp white pepper

dash of salt

clam-fry mixture (or equal parts cornmeal mixed with flour)

oil for deep frying

Ziggy's Ice Cream & Food

Ziggy's delightful little ice cream and food stand is a staple of Plymouth harbor. It's a fun place for kids *and* adults and has become a continuous part of Plymouth's spring and summer rituals. "I saw my first robin, the crocuses are blooming, and Ziggy's is open!"

Ziggy's is a sign of spring, the quintessential summer picnic by the sea. It's one of those places where everyone visits on a summer night for 50 flavors of ice cream, soft serve, and frozen yogurt; or stops by for a cheeseburger, fries, fried dough, or a luscious salmon burger. And, yes, there are often lines. That's what happens when you have a spotless restaurant, friendly, well-trained staff, choices galore, super service, and a billion dollar view. In fact, waiting in line gives you time to choose your favorite, re-think it, change your mind, and then order a large because you deserve it . . . with sprinkles.

And then you can sit down on a wooden bench or picnic table to enjoy your food and ice cream and watch the colorful world of summer pass by. You'll see a nightly parade of antique cars, hot rods, motorcycles, and a harbor full of sailboats, motor boats, and sight-seeing cruise ships.

Open from 11:00AM to 11:00PM, you'll find that Ziggy's shines morning, noon, and night. People flock there for a quick and tasty, quality lunch. They often finish it off with some homemade Richardson's ice cream. Frappes and milkshakes are good any time of the day, but especially good for cooling off the summer heat. Locals and tourists stop by in shorts and flip-flops and then settle in to an atmosphere that makes time stand still. Ziggy's brings back memories of childhood and the way that time runs slowly in summer and ice cream melts quickly.

Next time you're in the mood for something cold and crunchy, and just a little bit different, stop by Ziggy's for a Deep-Fried Ice Cream. Enjoy the recipe for this crunchy and creamy delight.

Ziggy's Ice Cream & Food

120 Water Street, Plymouth, MA 02360

Hours: Daily, 11:00AM–11:00PM

508-746-5411

Deep-Fried Ice Cream

DIRECTIONS

1. Scoop out a ball of your favorite ice cream. Wearing a pair of vinyl gloves, compact the ice cream in your hands. Pack it so that it is about the size of a baseball.

2. Proceed to roll the ice cream ball in crushed corn flakes (whole corn flakes will not stick well). You may add some cinnamon to the corn flakes if you like.

3. At this point, you want to roll your corn-flaked ice cream ball in the egg whites, and then repeat this process back into the crushed cinnamon/corn flakes. Your ice cream should be covered in corn flakes with the egg whites acting as a glue.

4. Place the ball of ice cream in a freezer for a few hours.

5. After a few hours, your ice cream ball should be frozen well, through and through. You now have a ball of your favorite ice cream ready for the fryer.

6. Heat your oil up to 360° in your deep fryer or wok. Take the ice cream ball(s) out of the freezer, and fry for just 15 seconds!

7. Drain on a paper towel for just a few seconds, and serve.

INGREDIENTS

ice cream of choice

corn flakes cereal, crushed

dash cinnamon (optional)

enough whisked egg whites to roll the ice cream ball(s) in

canola oil for deep frying

Cape Auto

THERE'S ALWAYS SOMETHING COOKIN' IN DAVE'S KITCHEN!

Dave Gallerani (left) and Greg Marinos (right).

Everybody in Plymouth knows that you can go to Cape Auto for honest, quality auto repair. For both vehicle service or auto body repairs, they are the best! But, did you know that Dave Gallerani and Greg Marinos prepare complimentary breakfast and lunch on a daily basis for the entire Cape Auto team? *Who does that?*

Dave is a third-generation owner at Cape Auto, while Greg is part of the Marinos clan that operated one of Plymouth's favorite restaurants for years, the iconic Colonial Restaurant on Main Street.

Who knows, if you are lucky enough to snag one of Cape Auto's coveted lunch-time repair slots the next time you schedule service online, you could find yourself sampling one of their culinary creations that keep their team rolling!

Dave and Greg have shared Cape Auto's recipe for Colonial Meatloaf in America's Hometown. Enjoy!

INGREDIENTS

2 lb ground meat of choice

1 green pepper, chopped

1 white onion, chopped

2 eggs, beaten

1 tsp black pepper

1 tsp garlic powder

2 tsp seasoning salt

1 T Italian seasoning

½ C bread crumbs

½ C grated Parmesan cheese

3 T Worcestershire sauce

6 T BBQ sauce

6 T ketchup

DIRECTIONS

Mix all ingredients together, pack well into one or two loaf pans (depending on size), and bake at 350° for 90 minutes.

Cape Auto Body & Service

Repairs: 53 Samoset Street, 508-746-0330

Collision: 115 Sandwich Street, 508-747-0316

Hours: Mon–Fri, 8:00AM–5:00PM

capeautorepairs.com

Proud community member of:

The Plymouth Area
CHAMBER OF COMMERCE
LEARN • CONNECT • SUCCEED

LIONS INTERNATIONAL

PLYMOUTH "THE ROCK"
BNI®

PLYMOUTH 400™
1620-2020
Business Partner

Beth Israel Deaconess Hospital
Plymouth
Community Business Partner

The Plymouth Cookbook is made possible by sponsorship from the businesses on the following pages, who continually support the community. Please take the time to read a bit about the products or services they offer.

❦

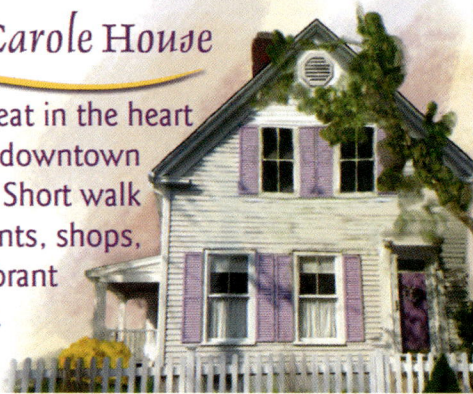

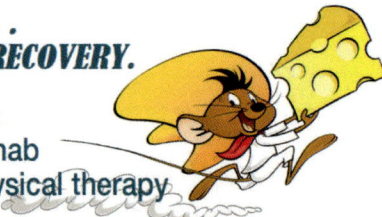

FOODIE FEDERATION

APPROVED

Index